Understanding the World Through Narrative

While many educational books focus on creative and critical thinking skills, this ground-breaking work is the first to deal specifically with the ability to understand, question and evaluate information presented, broadly speaking, in story form.

Story or narrative is central to our understanding of and interaction with the world around us. We only have to think of the 'mini stories' encapsulated in many advertisements; the way that topics in science – the story of human evolution for example, in history and other subjects present themselves; the power of myths and legends to act as guides to moral behaviour; and the pervasive way that gossip, rumour and superstition can spread – to recognise the benefits of heightening such awareness in young learners.

Understanding the World Through Narrative explores the narrative structure of fiction, but uses this as a template to show how the story form appears in mythology and modern urban folklore, science, history, the media – including advertising; in our internal dialogues (stories we tell ourselves about ourselves and others), and how narrative structure can be used in curriculum planning to enhance children's learning. The book contains over 160 thinking/discussing/researching activities for use in the classroom and as project work. Chapters can be used independently, although they are arranged with increasing degrees of sophistication and challenge. This fascinating work is an essential resource for any teacher of upper primary and lower secondary students, covering not only children's evolving intellectual ability and promoting curiosity and critical engagement but also enhancing their mental and emotional wellbeing.

Steve Bowkett began writing for pleasure in his teens and started to publish both fiction and educational books during his 20-year teaching career. He has so far published 81 titles. Since 1994, he has been a freelance fulltime writer, author visitor to hundreds of schools and an education consultant.

Tony Hitchman taught in primary schools for 35 years across the primary age range, culminating in 11 years as a primary head teacher. He has contributed artwork to a number of educational books/articles and has collaborated with Steve in creating three previous books published by Routledge.

Understanding the World Through Narrative

160+ Classroom Activities in Fiction, Mythology, Science, History, and the Media: StoryWise for 9–15 year-olds

Steve Bowkett and Tony Hitchman

LONDON AND NEW YORK

Designed cover image: © Getty Images
Cover illustrations: © Tony Hitchman

First published 2024
by Routledge
4 Park Square, Milton Park, Abingdon, Oxon OX14 4RN

and by Routledge
605 Third Avenue, New York, NY 10158

Routledge is an imprint of the Taylor & Francis Group, an informa business

© 2024 Steve Bowkett and Tony Hitchman

The right of Steve Bowkett and Tony Hitchman to be identified as authors of this work has been asserted in accordance with sections 77 and 78 of the Copyright, Designs and Patents Act 1988.

All rights reserved. No part of this book may be reprinted or reproduced or utilised in any form or by any electronic, mechanical, or other means, now known or hereafter invented, including photocopying and recording, or in any information storage or retrieval system, without permission in writing from the publishers.

Trademark notice: Product or corporate names may be trademarks or registered trademarks, and are used only for identification and explanation without intent to infringe.

British Library Cataloguing-in-Publication Data
A catalogue record for this book is available from the British Library

ISBN: 978-1-03252-896-0 (hbk)
ISBN: 978-1-03252-897-7 (pbk)
ISBN: 978-1-00340-903-8 (ebk)

DOI: 10.4324/9781003409038

Typeset in Sabon
by KnowledgeWorks Global Ltd.

Tony - To Sue - as always.

Steve - To Wendy, as ever.

In memory of my old friend Douglas Hill.

And to the past villains in my life, who've made me stronger.

Contents

List of figures   x

Introduction   1
Using the Book 5

1   Narrative Fiction   6

Story Pyramid 6
Narrative Elements 8
Narrative Elements as Archetypes 12
Sub-elements 13
Story 'Ingredients' 15
Genre 15
The Narrative Template 18
Characters 23
Names of People and Places 30
Nameplay 31
Place Names 32
Combi-town 34
Drives and Motivations 35
Emotions 35
Characters as Guides 36
Person 37
Fictional Genres 38
Tone, Atmosphere and the Spirit of Place 41
Twenty Questions 43
Story Checklist 44
Writing Effectively 45

2 Myths, Legends, Fairy Tales and Folklore 47

The Ladder to the Moon 52
Gossip and Rumours 52
Joseph Campbell 55
Legends, Fairy Tales and Folk Tales 58
A Controversy 59
A Hierarchy of Understandings 60
Wonderment and the Wisdom of Fairy Tales 62
Working with Grids 63
Folklore 68
Local Folktales 70
Urban Folk Tales 71
Rumours Revisited and Superstitions 75
Strength of Reasons 76
Superstitions 77
Thinking Critically 79

3 Scientific Narratives 82

Overview 82
Metaphors within Science 90
Falsifiability and Mumbo Jumbo 94
Fringe Science 98
Hoaxes 98

4 Historical Narratives 101

What Evidence? 101
Who Tells the Poor Man's Story? 101
The Attitudes of the Time 102
The Battle Narrative 103

5 Narratives in the Media 107

Ways to Persuade 107
The Issue of Truth 115
Conspiracy Theories 116
Clarity of Language 119
In the News 123

6 Therapeutic Stories — 127

Stories We Tell Ourselves 127
Visualising 129
Reframing 131
Inspiring Yourself 134

7 Stories and Learning — 138

Bloom's Taxonomy of Thinking 138
   Knowledge 139
   Comprehension 139
   Application 140
   Analysis 140
   Evaluation 140
   Synthesis 140
Related Thinking Skills 140
Reaching Conclusions 141
Relevant and Irrelevant Information 143
Crossing the Line 143
   The Double Darers Are 143
More Thinking Skills 154
   Noticing the Properties of Things; Attributing 154
   Noticing Similarities and Differences 154
   Categorising 154
   Comparing 155
   Ordering in Terms of Size 155
   Thinking about Concepts 156
   Abstract Concepts 158
   Generalising 159
   Decision-making 159
   Creative Consequences 160
Teaching as Storytelling 162
Effective Learners 164
   Endwords 168

Bibliography — 170
Index — 174

Figures

1.1	Story Pyramid.	7
1.2	Theme Card Examples.	9
1.3	Partners.	11
1.4	Sub-elements Grid.	13
1.5	Story Hill.	18
1.6	Infinity Symbol.	19
1.7	Infinity Symbol Numbered.	20
1.8	Character Profile.	25
1.9	Character Pyramid.	26
1.10	Vivid Particularities.	27
1.11	Narrative Heads.	28
1.12	Playing with Unafraid.	31
1.13	Place Name Generator.	33
1.14	Emotions and Storylines.	36
1.15	Form and Genre.	39
1.16	Stimulus for Lensing.	40
1.17	Twenty Questions Grid.	43
2.1	Ladder to the Moon.	53
2.2	Motifs Grids.	64
2.3	Stackers.	70
3.1	Science for Good or Ill.	84
3.2	Scientist Stereotypes.	85
3.3	The Narrative of Human Evolution.	93
4.1	Who Tells the Poor Man's Story?	102
4.2	The Battle Narrative.	104
4.3	Evolving Stories.	105
5.1	Stereotypes.	109
5.2	What We Don't Know.	109
6.1	White Light.	130
6.2	Whole Class Circle.	136
7.1	Contents of Bins.	142

Introduction

The word 'narrative' derives from Latin and means, variously; 'telling a story' and 'coming to know' ('story' itself has links with 'chronicle' and 'history'). Taking this second connotation, the concept of narrative goes beyond stories/fiction and can be applied in a wide range of contexts such as science, philosophy and religion – these perhaps being the three main areas of human curiosity and enquiry about ourselves, the universe and existence.

The highly respected biologist Edward O. Wilson in 'The Origins of Creativity' (Wilson, 2017) suggests that the talk among ancestral humans in the daytime focused on practical aspects of travel and the search for food and water, whereas at night, around the campfires, the talk turned to storytelling, frequently about successful hunts and epic adventures. Wilson quotes American author Elizabeth Marshall Thomas who, in 'The Old Way: a story of the first people' refers to the former hunter-gatherer Ju/'hoansi people of northeastern Namibia and the northwestern Kalahari Desert region of Botswana, whose firelight stories were commonly myth-like accounts of actual hunts. So as well as giving us one indication of the practical use and purpose of myth, it suggests that storytelling – the creation of narrative – has its roots thousands of years ago in the ancient past.

The notion of understanding is linked to the concept of intelligence (these words being etymologically connected). 'Intelligence' is a complex idea and has long been the focus of much psychological and educational research. Recent insights reveal that intelligence is not fixed and that it is not a single ability: people develop aptitudes in the way they think across a number of domains. A quick online search reveals that the neural plasticity of the brain (the fact that the brain changes over time) is reflected in changes of how the mind works and how learning occurs. Carol S. Dweck in 'Self Theories' (Dweck, 2000) has conducted research which indicates that if students believe that intelligence is fixed, then this seems to turn them towards concerns about performing and 'looking smart', whereas if students believe that intelligence is malleable, their concerns are focused more on learning new things and *getting* smarter:

In a nutshell, regarding intelligence as something dynamic and evolving drives learning.

Our primary intention when we first conceived this book was to focus on fiction, including children's own creative writing. And while we offer many activities that we hope will develop children's creative and critical thinking with regard to their own and others' writing, we soon realised that 'narratives' are embedded in science, in philosophy, in religion, in the media, in politics, in history and even in the 'stories' we tell ourselves; these having a powerful influence for good or ill on how we develop as human beings. We also include a section on myths, legends and folklore (including urban myths). While the word 'myth' is commonly taken to be something that is not true, strong arguments have been made that many myths communicate deep insights and truths that guide our moral behaviour – but more on that later. We also wanted to look at folklore/urban myths as these help children to gain insights into the proliferation of mis- and disinformation, relativism linked to truth and conspiracy theories that exist today, exacerbated by various social media platforms. As such the core themes of our book touch on – but are not the same as – information literacy. In both, the emphasis is on identifying, evaluating and applying sources of information. Also, both an awareness of narrative in different fields and information literacy promote thinking skills such as questioning, finding information, evaluating sources, seeking answers, making decisions and coming to conclusions.

Underpinning these thoughts, an important aim of what we're attempting to do is harness children's innate love of narrative to sharpen their thinking skills. We hope to begin to develop their powers of critical thinking, interpretation and analysis when presented with information in a variety of contexts. Instead of the children being passive and unquestioning recipients of 'facts', we hope to encourage an open, perceptive and reflective approach to enhance children's understanding and begin to develop the vitally important thinking skills that are essential to their future development.

So it was that as our research continued, the idea of 'narrative' broadened out to include these other realms of enquiry. The subject therefore became too large to cover thoroughly all of the areas of narrative that we mention. We hope, though, that as well as offering practical activities in all of them, we also point the way to other resources that you can access if your interest and programmes of study with the children take you in that particular direction. (We were interested to note as we explored the subject, narrative awareness also plays a part in the evolution of artificially intelligent [AI] computers. We also found references to the power of storytelling in articles on leadership and charisma in the business world, though we've not touched on these.)

From time to time, we insert paragraphs on a personal note, switching to the first person, in which we offer examples from our own lives of how narrative, used in the broader sense as defined above, has influenced us ...

Steve – I have vivid memories of reenacting scenes from the 1963 film 'Jason and the Argonauts' with my friends. Because I was the tallest in the group, I had to be the bronze giant Talos, guardian of the treasure-house of the gods and invariably defeated by the hero Jason (played in turn by my other mates). This reenactment of 'narrative fragments' of the Jason story allowed our group to come to a deeper understanding, albeit perhaps tacitly, of heroism, taboos, 'stepping over the line', the supernatural (and hence implicitly what counts as 'real'), the notion of deity and other themes directly or not so directly relevant to ordinary life.

As the educationalist Margaret Meek asserts, storytelling, including through play, pervades our explanations, hopes, fears, dreams and plans (Meek, 1991); or as Don Watson says in his book 'Gobbledygook' (Watson, 2005) 'story' acts as a frame of reference for what we experience in our lives.

Children often then develop their own adventures based on existing characters or scenarios. Thus, in the wonderful world of superheroes, Superman can fight it out with the Hulk to see who is stronger (it depends how angry the Hulk is!); Peppa Pig's family or the Sylvanian Folk can get up to all sorts of antics and, through choose-your-own-adventure books and a whole multitude of games, children can be active participants in developing their own narratives within a given scenario or, increasingly, building their own unique imagined worlds.

When playing, young children are constantly developing or working through ideas or situations, some based on mundane events such as cooking in the home corner; others based on fantasies, perhaps a dinosaur tea party. Children's early drawings can also have a narrative quality with characters, objects and situations added as they come to mind ... 'They're having a picnic and teddy is with them – but look there's a black cloud'. Scenarios from lived experience are constantly being supplemented by ideas from stories, television, films and games, often combining elements from diverse sources. All of this leads to the conclusion that any person's reality is a complex interweaving of the external world and the internal world of the imagination: the philosopher Colin Wilson asserted that most people live 90% of the time in their own heads. And while as teachers we educate children to be confident, capable and safe in the outside world, we think it's equally important to show children how to use their ability to organise and analyse experience – to recognise the narrative structure of their world – as intelligently as possible.

Activity: Depending upon the age of the children, ask them if they play in the sense of reenacting stories and/or what memories they have of doing that. Apart from being fun, what else do the children gain or learn from such play?

Early play, then, often evolves into a complex mixing of fiction and what we take to be factual events, both subsumed into that slippery concept of 'reality'.

Steve – I was in my teens as the 1970s ended. My favourite author was Arthur C. Clarke, my favourite TV programme was the Gerry Anderson series 'UFO' and I was hugely excited by NASA's ongoing Apollo moonshot program. All of these influences filled me with a deep sense of optimism, a vision of the future that was ripe with possibilities and opportunities. Arthur C. Clarke's science fiction is laced with accounts of amazing technology and of human expansion through the galaxy. The Apollo missions were a real-life example of that, albeit a small first step (but a giant leap for mankind!). In 'UFO', a secret lunar installation acts as first line of defence against alien attack. Flights from the Earth to the Moon and back are routine. The heady mix of these things had a mythic quality insofar as they acted as templates for how I felt and how I thought about my ambitions at that liminal point in my life between childhood and adulthood.

In his book 'The Limitations of Scientific Truth' (Brush, 2005), the American geologist Nigel Brush quotes from cognitive scientist Mark Turner's 'The Literary Mind'. Turner asserts that 'story' is the fundamental instrument of thought and that rational capacities depend on it as our chief means of envisioning, of predicting and deciding, and of explaining. In short, narratives shape our thought and create the lenses through which we perceive the world.

Before we get started on narrative fiction, here are a few more activities …

Ask the children if they own anything that is important to them and why; toys, books they love, holiday mementoes, pictures, etc. Because these things are precious, they can be used as a doorway into discussions about not just what we value, but the idea of values more generally and how these influence our behaviour. Author Simon Danser in his 'The Myths of Reality' (Danser, 2005) asserts that reality is significantly about the meanings we give to things. He goes on to suggest that our personal meanings are fed by multiple messages from the culture in which we are embedded. This can open up discussion further to explore society's effect on what we value.

Ask the children to define what 'precious' means and to think about things that are precious to them (they don't need to mention these). Can stories be precious? And if so, in what sense?

As an ongoing activity through the book, ask children to look up the etymology of relevant words such as; story, narrative, myth, fable, folktale, science, philosophy, truth, etc. Have them use a variety of dictionaries if possible to pick up different wordings and nuances. Can they construct their own definitions based on these? Get them to look in a thesaurus for synonyms and consider whether the offerings are indeed synonymous. For instance, looking up 'narrative' in our very battered copy of Roget's Thesaurus we're offered; plot, sub-plot, scenario, history, chronicle, legend, myth, allegory, parable, fiction, yarn and many others – a rich field here for discussion!

Another benefit of exploring etymology is that often you'll find a little story – a mini narrative – behind the word. For instance, the word 'vaccination' derives from the Latin *vacca*, meaning cow. The story behind this is that in the 1790s, the English physician Edward Jenner noticed that dairymaids who had been infected by cowpox did not catch smallpox; cowpox being a much milder disease and readily survivable. Jenner developed the technique of vaccination by taking fluid from the dairymaids' cowpox pustules and deliberately infected children through a small wound in the skin. In 1853, a law was passed requiring universal vaccination against smallpox in England and Wales. Vaccines for other diseases were then developed and became a standard technique long before the human immune system was described in detail.

It's not a great stretch of the imagination to see how even a small narrative such as this one maps on to the basic narrative template, as described on page 18. The story also gives insight into the history of medical science and, we think, serves as a 'vivid particularity' (page 26) insofar as it stimulates the imagination and delivers a certain emotional impact which, as teachers, we know that makes facts more memorable. The tale also serves as a way of debating the ongoing controversy about vaccines, touching as it does on the notion of conspiracy theories, which we look at in Chapter 5.

Using the Book

The different sections are loosely sequenced in terms of conceptual difficulty. Thus, working through the book section by section we hope develops children's understanding of narrative structure as it moves from fiction through to myth and legend, history, science, the media and therapeutic stories. We end with a section on how narrative structure, including fictional stories, can be used as a model for curriculum planning.

However, the sections are also to some extent self-contained. Because you may wish to look at sections separately, or only use some of them, we've repeated salient points in these different units of the book.

Another alternative is to cherry pick the thinking/discussion/research activities (there are around 160 of them) and build them in to your own programmes of study.

* * *

1 Narrative Fiction

According to vocabulary.com (accessed November 2021), the word fiction is linked to the Latin *fictus*, meaning 'to form', since fiction is formed in the imagination. There is a philosophical issue here, insofar as all human concepts (based on human perceptions of the external world) are formed in the imagination. The point also needs to be made that fictional stories, such as parables and fairy tales, can *tell us something true*. Steve reminds children of this on his school visits, since many children seem to hold the simplistic belief that fiction is made up and not true, while facts are things that have been discovered about the world and the universe, and are true (often without questioning what 'true' could mean). One of the purposes of this book is to highlight the idea that fiction can be true in various ways, while facts are tentative and should always be checked, at least if important decisions in life are to be based on them. Elsewhere, the Oxford Languages website tells us that the word fiction derives from Latin terms meaning to 'form' or 'contrive'. 'Form' itself seems a neutral term, since facts too are formed in the mind, as just mentioned; the word 'fact' being linked etymologically with 'factory' and 'manufacture' – formed by humans. 'Contrive' means to be created deliberately, rather than arising naturally or spontaneously.

Story Pyramid

However, this aside, one way of giving children insight into the structure of narrative fiction is to show them what we call the story pyramid (Figure 1.1), which shows the hierarchical nature of narrative.

The foundations of a story are its themes (from the Greek for 'proposition' and related to *tithenai* meaning to 'set' or 'place' – you might ask the children how these ideas fit with the notion of themes in a story); the underpinning points, foci or topics of a story.

Steve – I had been writing fiction for years before I realised, in my later teens, that I had been building my stories on the same handful of themes, and that these related to my own life. They included –

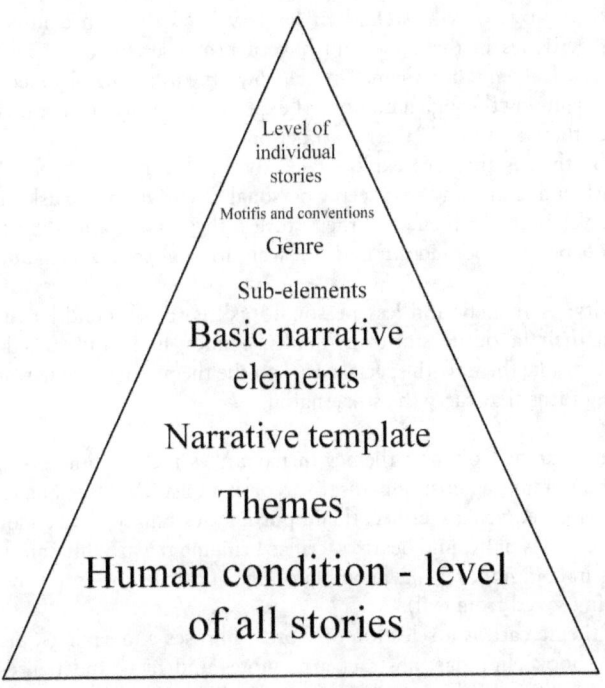

Figure 1.1 Story Pyramid.

Crossing the line, testing the rules, going into forbidden territory (Cf. my reference to 'Jason and the Argonauts' on page 3 and the exemplar story 'Crossing the Line' on page 143). As a child, if I did something moderately naughty, my mother would deal with me and mete out the punishment. If my misdemeanour was more serious, I'd have to face my father. On several occasions I remember him, grim-faced, pointing at me and saying, 'You've stepped over the line this time, my lad'. A real-life theme explored later through story.

The problems that come with sudden power. My chosen genres for writing stories were and still are Fantasy, Science Fiction and Horror, so the notion of acquiring sudden power took on various incredible forms such as magic, the power to shape-shift, time travelling, etc. Again this theme related to my life insofar as, I suppose, like many children I felt powerless in all kinds of situations.

Being heroic and getting the girl. Plenty of adolescent wishful thinking here!

Activity: Now, or when children have worked through a number of other activities in the book and have a firmer grasp of the idea of a theme, ask them if any themes in their own life (identified by a common thread running through a number of experiences) echo the themes in any stories they know, or in their own fiction.

The themes that are explored in stories, therefore, can be subconsciously influential and also deeply personal. If you choose to ask children to think about the themes in their stories, they may want to keep their insights private and, indeed, may not want to think about them at all.

Activity: A related, and less personal, task is to ask children to think about their favourite stories in books, comics, films and to reflect on why they like them, with special focus on the themes of those narratives – the big ideas that carry the stories along.

Theme Cards: Common themes in narratives include humans against nature, humans against humans, overcoming obstacles, learning lessons, friendship requiring sacrifice, the importance of family, love conquering all, the cycles of life and death, sacrifice bringing reward, humans having needs in common, revenge, coming of age and redemption (in the sense of being saved from evil).

A theme card is a selection of words, phrases and sayings, pictures, comic book clippings, abstract art, quotes and facts and figures used to highlight and help describe a theme. Individual children, or children working in small groups, can create such a display on an A4 sheet of card, or the whole class can work on a larger presentation. Laminated theme cards form a permanent resource to use with other classes.

Note: If you feel that the traditional literary themes above are too adult or complex for the children, select some proverbs that indicate themes and/or ask groups to choose a favourite story and 'generalise it out' to create a theme card, as in this example, that can be used as the basis for other plot ideas (Figure 1.2).

Narrative Elements

If themes are the foundations of stories, then narrative elements form their main building blocks. Traditionally, these are –
The hero or protagonist (from Greek words meaning 'first in importance' and 'actor'), whose job is to resolve a problem and restore harmony and balance to the world. Usually, a hero will personify 'noble' qualities (i.e. display high moral standards) such as courage, compassion and kindness, among others – though a *completely* good hero can be boring. One indication that heroes are ordinary human beings is that often they will resist the 'call to action' and be reluctant to get

Narrative Fiction 9

Figure 1.2 Theme Card Examples.

involved. More interesting heroes will also have other flaws or weaknesses too ...

Steve – My favourite comic book heroes were (are, let's be honest) Spiderman and Batman. Spiderman (as Peter Parker) had concerns over money, worried about his aged Aunt May (in the comics she was elderly), was too shy across many stories to ask Gwen Stacey or Mary Jane Watson for a date and sometimes came down with a twenty-four hour virus so that he had to face villains in a weakened state. Batman in his Dark Knight incarnation seemed psychologically fractured at times, while Gotham City itself grew darker and more violent than in earlier versions of Batman. Batman's sidekick Robin was introduced in the 1940s to soften the rather grim persona of the Batman and to make him more fatherly and approachable. Significantly, Robin was sent off to college when the 1970s Batman started to grow darker. There is also a contrast between Batman as a dark revenge figure and the benevolent god myth embodied by Superman and the redemptive and empowerment aspect of Wonder Woman.

The villain (Latin, a low born rustic or farmhand – children can do some research and find out how this links to villainy) or antagonist (Greek, 'to struggle against') creates the story's central problem or problems. In the same way that a totally good hero is dull, so a completely evil villain is similarly uninteresting. Many children cast villains in their own stories as simply 'mad', which is a very weak motivation for their actions. A more convincing villain, one that the reader can better relate to, will have at least one redeeming feature, or at least indications of one through a backstory. Having said this, Doctor Who's greatest enemies, the Daleks, are portrayed as completely evil in most of their stories and are still wreaking havoc since their first appearance over sixty years ago. Also, thinking again of the Batman 'mythoverse', the chilling aspect of Batman's arch enemy, the Joker (in some of his incarnations), is his complete lack of logic or sanity: other villains such as Superman's Lex Luthor can be portrayed as evil but be the hero of the narrative in their own minds. It's interesting to note too that an alien like Superman with the powers of a god could conceivably be a danger to the human species.

(Much more information on the hero, the villain and the other story elements can be found in 'Developing Thinking Skills Through Creative Writing', Bowkett & Hitchman, 2020).

Problem. The tension and conflict in a story arise through the narrative's central problem. Other subsidiary problems might stem from this. The problem is often caused by the villain's desire for wealth, power or revenge, among other motives.

Journey. This idea can be viewed in two ways. Often in stories (especially longer quest stories), the hero and his friends will literally set out on a journey to dangerous realms (see the narrative template on page 18). But 'journey' can also mean a transformative experience brought about by what the hero has endured. Note however that villains can be transformed too, a well-known example being Darth Vader's turning away from the dark side in the Star Wars saga.

Partner. Heroes and villains often have partners and sidekicks. A partner is more than a subsidiary character. The hero's sidekick can highlight his/her flaws and weaknesses, while the villain's partner can be linked to the antagonist's redeeming feature(s). Sidekicks can also be sent on missions of their own, so creating the opportunity for subplots. In many stories, villainous figures can form a 'hierarchy'. Again referring to Star Wars, Darth Vader is the films' main villain, though he is subservient to the Emperor.

Activity: Ask the children to come up with some examples of partners from stories they've enjoyed. Can they identify the functions of the partner in the narrative?

Activity: Often the protagonist is partnered with an older character who acts as a mentor who aids and teaches them. Examples include Obi Wan Kenobi and Luke Skywalker, Batman and Robin, Mr Miyagi and Daniel in the 'Karate Kid' or Balloo who teaches Mowgli the ways of the forest in 'The Jungle Book'. Ask children to look at the illustration, of possible

Figure 1.3 Partners.

partners in Figure 1.3, list some motifs – constituent details – that identify the genre, and suggest how the partner might be able to help the protagonist in each case.

Help. This is an important element insofar as it demonstrates that any of the characters can encounter difficulties in their role or mission, therefore making them more believable and heightening tension. Help can come in the form of other characters, happenstance/coincidence (though this should not be overused), while in horror and fantasy stories, help might come from a supernatural source.

Knowledge and Power. This takes the form of the gaining and losing of advantage through the narrative. Again, the children can probably come up with lots of examples. This element is closely linked with varying the tension in a story, which in turn is connected to other aspects of the narrative such as pace and atmosphere.

Object. This element, like Journey, can be viewed in two ways. It can refer to a physical object that might need to be recovered, returned to its rightful owner or place or even destroyed because it is so potentially dangerous (Cf. Lord of the Rings). Desiring an object can give the villain motivation, while recovering the object supplies a strong reason for the hero's journey and willingness to face danger. The word can also be read as 'objective'; the hero's aim in the story, which broadly speaking is to resolve the problem(s) created by the villain. (Note that resolve – re-solve – means to solve again. One feature of the human condition is that good and evil will always exist: there will always be villains causing problems and there will always be the need for heroes to try to resolve them. Again, refer to the narrative template on page 18. The psychotherapist Kim Schneiderman in 'Step Out of Your Story' (Schneiderman, 2015) asserts that stories 'push towards a resolution', applying the idea to our desire to resolve issues in our own lives. We'll return to this notion in the section 'Therapeutic Stories'.)

Narrative Elements as Archetypes

According to the ideas of the Swiss psychiatrist Carl Jung, an archetype is an ancient mental image, common across all cultures, that we inherit from our early ancestors. Archetypes are theorised to exist in what Jung calls the collective unconscious, a level of mentality below that of the personal subconscious; a realm common to all human minds.

In 'The Origins of Creativity' (Wilson, 2017), biologist E. O. Wilson takes up this idea, suggesting that the basic narrative elements have an archetypal quality stemming from prehuman and primitive human times, many thousands of years ago.

The hero fights alone or rallies support against, at first, seemingly insurmountable odds. Wilson also identifies the tragic hero (a sub-element perhaps, see the following section), who possesses a fatal flaw that leads to the hero's downfall and even to the destruction of the tribe. Wilson points out that all through history many of the mighty have risen only to fall.

The Monster (one aspect of the villain) as a narrative element supposedly derives from pre- and protohuman fear of large predators. Interestingly, the word monster comes from the Latin for 'portent' and 'warning'.

The quest/journey has its origins in the fact that our early ancestors were hunter-gatherers, constantly in search of food. Discoveries of drinkable water sources, animals and edible plants were literally a matter of life and death. Wilson suggests that such journeyings were the source of many of these early tribes' stories and legends.

Wilson also identifies the pair bond as a vital archetype. This may refer to the notion of the partner, though heroes (increasingly not just the male) battle against the odds to win the affections of another. Also, men and women may join forces in a fight for freedom, reflecting the necessity in ancient tribes for altruism and cooperation.

The archetype of 'other worlds' refers to new, unknown and possibly dangerous realms – see the narrative template on page 18. Hunter-gatherer tribes would constantly be encountering new 'realms'. Wilson takes the idea back over 60,000 years to the 'African breakout' of human groups as they spread to other areas of the globe. Encountering other tribes might be likened to challenges encountered at the liminal point between the known and the unknown; the 'threshold guardian' appearing in the form of natural obstacles and/or hostile tribes.

In his book, E. O. Wilson cites many well-known films where these archetypes form necessary elements of the stories' narrative cohesion and emotional power; though any number of successful children's books would serve the same function if used in the classroom. The points to be taken from Wilson's suggestions are that narrative elements go way,

way back into human prehistory, are still active today in the real world and widely reflected in fiction, indicating that the 'building blocks' of narrative are constantly reimagined across all cultures and thus serve as an ongoing social/cultural force.

Sub-elements

The folklorist Vladimir Propp in his 'Morphology of the Folktale' (Propp, 2001) identified a number of sub-elements in his examination of traditional folktales; variations of the major elements that we've just looked at. We've used some of these (in Figure 1.4), tweaked some and added a few, to create our sub-elements grid.

Activities: Ask children to cast their eyes across the grid as a whole and identify any sub-elements they recognise from stories they know.

Can children recognise any sub-elements that feature in their own lives? Note that some children may not want to do this if it might evoke unpleasant memories. Or they may prefer to keep their insights strictly private.

Steve – A hero appeared in my life when Doctor Who began on TV in 1963. In the 1990s, a 'villain' attempted to lever me out of my job. The issue was resolved by my quitting the job to embark on a writing career, and in that sense the villain was defeated ('the best revenge is

Moving from familiar territory.	The villain attempts deceit.	The hero is tested.	The villain escapes.	The hero goes unrecognised.	The hero is recognised.
An instruction is given or implied.	The hero or victim is deceived.	Help appears.	The villain is defeated.	A false hero appears.	The false hero is exposed.
A rule is broken.	The villain causes harm or injury.	The hero acquires power.	A situation is resolved.	The false hero deceives.	The hero has a different appearance.
The villain appears.	Misfortune appears.	The hero goes to a new place.	The hero returns.	A difficult task is proposed.	The villain escapes.
The consequences of breaking a rule.	A request is made or command given.	Hero and villain meet in direct conflict.	The hero is pursued.	The task is undertaken	The villain is punished.
The villain gains information on the hero.	The hero decides to act.	The hero is 'marked'.	The hero is rescued.	The task succeeds or fails.	The hero is rewarded.

Figure 1.4 Sub-elements Grid.

living well', attributed to the 16th-century poet George Herbert). Our values – a sense of fairness and justice for example – are influenced by both real and fictional heroes and people/characters that we warm to and admire. In other words, make-believe can and often does help us to 'make beliefs' that feed the values through which we live our lives.

Based on stories they know, can the children think of any further sub-elements? Would they replace any on the grid with their own ideas?

Use dice-rolls to choose two sub-elements at random – 'along the corridor and up the stairs'. Can children now think of a 'seed story' – a story idea expressed in one sentence – by linking the sub-elements? Examples include –

1–6 Moving from familiar territory/3–4 A situation is resolved. A character is having trouble with neighbours and moves away.

3–2 The hero goes to a new place/The hero or victim is deceived. Coincidentally, this can be linked with the idea above. The character who becomes the unwitting or unwilling hero of the story goes to a new location and is befriended by a new neighbour who subsequently deceives him/her.

3–6 The hero is tested/4–4 The villain is defeated. These are standard aspects of a story, which still leaves a gap in the middle ...

6–3 The hero has a different appearance/6–1 The villain is punished. The hero uses disguise to thwart the villain, who through his/her own deceitfulness receives their just deserts.

Using a 6 × 6 grid and dice rolls brings randomness into the creative process. This encourages children to 'think on their feet', hopefully steering them away from clichéd and predictable storylines. You can see that after four sets of dice rolls, a possible storyline is emerging. It isn't genre specific, although children can choose a genre before they begin the activity. There aren't a set number of dice rolls: some children will evolve a workable storyline after a few, while others will need to keep going before they develop a rounded idea. Children can also change the sequence of the ideas the dice rolls throw up to suit their evolving thoughts.

Another benefit of 6 × 6 grids is that children can create their own, fitting just words into the cells, or images that they draw or cut from comics, etc., or a mixture. Grids can also be based on a child's favourite story. Once a grid has been prepared, all the information is 'visually available', so that as a child looks at it, however glancingly, further creative connections can be made spontaneously even as the child goes through the more formal process of dice rolling. A giant grid can also be prepared as a group or whole-class project. In some schools where we've worked, several classes each created a giant grid and then swapped, so that each class had the opportunity to work with fresh ideas.

For further details on using randomness within the creative process, see 'Visualising Literacy and How to Teach It' (Bowkett & Hitchman, 2022), while more grids are featured in our book 'Developing Thinking Skills Through Creative Writing' (Bowkett & Hitchman, 2020).

Story 'Ingredients'

These are aspects of narrative that add flavour and texture to a story (hence the culinary metaphor). They include secrets, conflicts, dangers, mysteries, humour and treasures (something precious). Pace, tone, tension and atmosphere can also be included. All of these constitute what, in our opinion, are subtler aspects of narrative than are plot, characters and settings, though all of these features work together to create the story dynamic.

Activity: One way of highlighting the notion of what we're calling ingredients is to pose a number of questions and ask children to re-examine stories they know to find the answers. So, for example –

What does the author do to make a story scary?
How can you tell that there's action in a story so that the plot moves along quickly?
What dangerous situations do characters find themselves in from stories you know?
How do authors who write comedic stories make them funny?
How do you know a story is a mystery tale?
Can you think of any precious objects that appear in stories you've read?

Genre

The word 'genre' derives from early 19th-century French and means literally 'a kind' (the word is also linked to genre from the Latin genus meaning 'birth, family, nation' – Oxford Languages). There's a huge literature on writing genre fiction, most of it directed at adult authors. Our own 'Developing Thinking Skills Through Creative Writing' (Bowkett & Hitchman, 2020) covers many aspects of writing by focusing on a different genre in each chapter. For our purposes here – in explaining where genre fits into the story pyramid – we'll mention just a few points that we think are relevant.

Each genre will have its own motifs and conventions. Motifs are the constituent features of a genre, the smaller particular details that help to define and describe that genre. So taking Science Fiction as an example, a typical story might contain spacecraft, distant worlds, aliens, beam weapons and so on. Conventions are the aspects of a story, including characters, settings and key events that are commonly found in any particular genre, though overused conventions become clichés. Ideally, young writers working within a genre are familiar with it; so a child who wants to create a fantasy tale will do so most effectively if she is familiar with the motifs and conventions of Fantasy.

More experienced young writers, once they are confident in using a genre's motifs and conventions, can experiment with using them more *un*conventionally. One aspect of this is to take motifs from two different genres and mix them within a story. So vampires in space or a time travelling wizard, etc.

Some aspects of story, such as romance, thriller and comedy, form genres in their own right, but can also serve as story 'ingredients' as described earlier, to flavour and texture a story within a chosen genre. So a fantasy story can feature romance, a horror tale can feature comedy and so on. (Writing comedic horror is difficult to do well – all the more reason for encouraging any young writer who wants to try!)

Even though genres like Science Fiction, Horror and Fantasy are fantastical (as in unreal or fanciful), stories set within them need to be logically consistent. That is to say, the world of the story should be supported by robust rationales and the absence of logical contradictions. These make the created world more believable. One common feature of many stories we've come across featuring magic, for instance, is that there's no explanation or reasoning behind its existence or use. A wizard points his fingers or a wand and magic comes out. Now it may be the case that children simply want to have fun writing and aren't concerned about logical consistency, which is fine. Those who wish to pursue their writing skills further, however, should at some point give the matter additional thought. Magic having no limitations creates its own problems; if it can be used in any situation to do anything, where is the drama? Perhaps it can only be used on inanimate objects, requires intense concentration, can be used up, has serious drawbacks or only works with a certain talisman. And with regard to Fantasy and Science Fiction (SF), it has been wisely said that a good fantasy story makes the impossible seem possible, while a good science fiction story makes the possible seem probable, in part because of the logical consistency and hence greater believability of the tale.

Steve – Coincidentally, during the writing of this section I watched a superhero movie one afternoon. Towards the end, as the climax unfolded, the major villain shut down all mobile and landline networks as part of his attack. The point of view was with the hero and subsidiary 'good guys' in this scene. Before dashing off to pursue the villain, the hero told one of the minor characters to contact the authorities, which this person did immediately – using a mobile phone. Many viewers perhaps would not have noticed this, but people who do might be jolted out of the narrative by the contradiction. It may well be of course that the scriptwriters did it deliberately to avoid complicating the narrative or using extra footage of minor characters leaving the building to find a police station or a working phone, so that the action and pace are maintained. In film and TV, because of their very kinetic nature, the audience can be bowled along by the narrative and not notice such inconsistencies, whereas text authors are not so lucky – their readers can refer back to check.

A related point is the use of 'pseudoscience' (pseudo from Middle English meaning 'false or spurious'). For instance, in Doctor Who, the analogue of the wizard's wand is the famous sonic screwdriver. According to Wikipedia, it made its first appearance in 1968 in the story 'Fury From the Deep' featuring the actor Patrick Troughton as the Doctor's second incarnation. It's gotten the Doctor out of many tight spots since then! Pseudoscience in genre fiction can also take the form of gobbledygook – meaningless language, or language that becomes unintelligible through the use of technical terms. We touch on pseudoscience purporting to be 'real' science on page 95.

Steve – My favourite Doctor (third incarnation) was played by Jon Pertwee between 1970 and 1974. Two pseudoscientific sentences in particular that he used became famous; 'reverse the polarity of the neutron flow' was a sure fire way of stopping some device from exploding, while 'I think there's a small fault in the interstitial beam synthesiser' pinpointed the reason why some machine or other wasn't working. Reversing the polarity of the neutron flow usually cleared the fault.

Some genres can be split into smaller sub-genres. SF for example can be broken down into space opera featuring epic warfare in space (a la Star Wars), time travel tales, parallel worlds, cyberpunk and others. Fantasy stories might be set in other worlds or dimensions, or the magic might arise within our normal everyday world. Horror stories can be subdivided into gothic horror, tales featuring the paranormal, so-called body or gory horror (not suitable for children we think, though many youngsters might disagree), post-apocalyptic tales and others. A quick online search will bring up further examples.

Motifs, which we've already looked at briefly, add another level of detail and specificity to the story pyramid. Although the term is commonly used to mean a prominent feature recurring in an artistic or dramatic work, we think the idea becomes clearer for children by using the analogy of textiles, where a motif is a pattern of stitching that gives a garment its individuality. The metaphor also supports the etymological link between 'textiles' and 'text', from the Latin for 'woven'. Thus, we talk of weaving a tale, spinning a yarn, following a plot thread and gathering material prior to writing.

Activity: Ask the children how they know that a story they're familiar with is a fantasy story or a horror story, or whatever genre they choose. Create a list of motifs (and conventions if any are suggested). Separate out the motifs into the categories of plot, characters and settings. This takes us to the peak of the story pyramid, the level of individual tales.

The Narrative Template

Many if not most children will know about the 'story hill', as in Figure 1.5, as a visual planning tool for narrative. Exposition or setting the scene is followed by a crises caused by the story's central problem, which in turn – as tension rises – leads to conflict between the protagonist, antagonist and other characters. The climax of the story comes in the final confrontation between hero and villain, following which there is a rounding off of the narrative in light of the problem's resolution.

Incidentally, in her self-help book 'Step Out of Your Story', psychotherapist Kim Schneiderman uses the story hill analogy within the context of resolving personal issues. We'll return to that in the section 'Therapeutic Stories'.

Figure 1.5 Story Hill.

Narrative Fiction 19

Figure 1.6 Infinity Symbol.

A more sophisticated, and in our opinion more useful, visual metaphor makes use of the mathematical symbol for infinity, as shown in Figure 1.6.

Activity: Explain to the children that the left lobe of the image represents 'our world', the world of the hero's ordinary life and experience. The right hand lobe represents a new and unknown realm of danger, tension and conflict. Based on what the children have learned about the basic narrative elements, ask them how the infinity image could help them to use the elements to plan a story.

Whatever the children's response, you can go on to flesh out their ideas. Figure 1.7 shows significant steps through a story.

1 The opening of the story sets the scene (the hero's everyday world) and introduces the hero and other relevant characters.
2 Shortly afterwards there comes what is traditionally known as the 'call to action'. The problem becomes known, or intimations of it at least, and the hero realises he or she must become involved. Traditionally, the hero is reluctant to get drawn in to the world of conflict and danger.
3 However, for whatever reason (perhaps tied in with the protagonist's noble qualities), the hero must begin the journey – literally and as a transformative experience – in an attempt to resolve the issue. Notice that the diagram portrays this as a descent; perhaps as a going-down towards danger in the unknown, or maybe a draining of the hero's confidence, or both. Having the hero doubt his/her own abilities humanises the character and helps us to identify with them.
4 Here the hero crosses over into the realm of danger and new experience. In traditional tales – and in many myths and legends – here the

20 *Narrative Fiction*

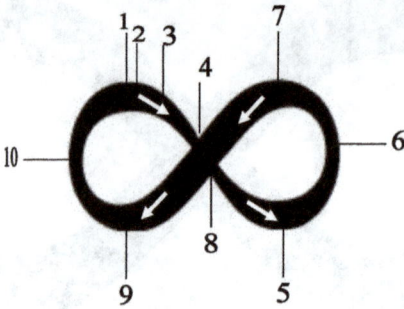

1 - Call to action
2 - Resisting the call
3 - First brush with danger
4 - Crossing the threshold to the other realm
5 - Point of lowest ebb
6 - Point of greatest threat
7 - Point of false hope / calm before the storm
8 - Recrossing the threshold / further crisis
9 - A twist in the tale
10 - Problem resolved / rounding off.

Figure 1.7 Infinity Symbol Numbered.

hero must face a first significant challenge in the form of a 'threshold guardian'. This might come in the form of another character, a situation or perhaps some inner conflict. It is at this point often that the hero begins to draw on previously unsuspected inner resources.

5 Even though the hero overcomes the threshold challenge, a further descent into danger is inevitable, and it looks as though our protagonist's morale can sink no lower. This point in the story often features further trials where the hero might lose all hope of resolving the issue or even of surviving.

6 However, the inner resources that emerged earlier reassert themselves and it seems that progress is being made. Notice though that the visual causes us to realise that the hero is now deep into the villain's domain and as far away from home as it's possible to be.

7 After further adventures, things seem to be 'on the up'. This phase of the story is sometimes called 'the point of false hope' …

8 Because soon afterwards, the hero is plunged into a fresh crisis in the form of another threshold guardian. The word crisis incidentally comes from the Latin and originally meant the turning point in a disease. The connotation of a crisis being a 'decisive point' emerged in the 17th century (Oxford Languages).

9 Note that although the hero has now returned to his or her familiar world, danger is still present, leading to a further low ebb. This might take the form of a 'twist in the tale', a final shock or threat before resolution of the problem occurs.
10 Here we have the story's ending or denouement; the final scene(s) where any loose ends are tied up and the resolution is fully and finally realised; though some stories end with a further possible threat if a sequel is planned.

Activity: Ask the children to think of a story they like and see how well the plot maps onto the narrative template. Many highly popular and successful stories do map closely. Point out to the class that the infinity symbol reinforces the idea that the battle between good and evil is eternal; that there will always be villains causing problems, creating the need for heroes to face the challenges to resolve them. Such is the human condition.

As an adjunct to this, even the most fantastical stories, dealing as many do with the eternal battle between good and evil, tell children 'something true' about the real world and can help to shape their moral landscape and sense of values from an early age. Linked to this are the timeless 'rhetorical traditions' in storytelling, principally 'once upon a time', 'once long ago', and 'they all lived happily ever after'. George Lucas, the creator of the Star Wars universe, recognised this when the opening credits – the 'crawl text' – of Star Wars episode IV begin with the words 'A long time ago in a galaxy far away' (we checked this on the wonderfully named Wookieepedia website). There is a certain irony here insofar as in real life our 'battles' against unfairness, injustice, deceit, etc., when they appear are faced in the here-and-now.

Activities: Ask children to decide on a genre, choose some motifs from the grids on page 64, then 'translate' them into the selected genre. So if we choose SF, guardian might be a robot, city could be an alien city and talisman might translate into a device for opening doors (such as Doctor Who's sonic screwdriver). If we choose Fantasy, then disguise might be a creature that can transform, egg might be a dragon's egg and alphabet might translate into some esoteric language or runic symbols.

Ask children to choose a theme – good versus evil for instance – and, using some of their chosen motifs, think about how they might be used in a story exploring the theme they've selected. If possible, can they sum up the storyline in a short paragraph?

Again using the motif grids on page 64, ask children to use dice rolls to choose ten motifs at random, placing one at each of the significant points on the narrative template. A storyline (albeit within the fantasy genre) might grow from this. If not, encourage children to use the counter flip game (page 29), working on one motif at a time, to generate more information and prompt further ideas.

Steve – I was amused but not surprised to realise that even some gameshows map on to the narrative template to a large degree. After a hard day's writing on Saturday I was chilling out with my wife watching the UK's 'The Wall' and 'The Wheel', and it wasn't difficult to pick out the problem (the random nature of the game – can also be viewed as the villain); the hero (contestants); the 'villain' in the form of getting questions wrong/losing money; the partner in the form of the host; the journey towards finally winning or losing; help in the form of celebrity guests (in 'The Wheel'); knowledge/power in how much the contestants and celebrities know and how that can get them closer to winning; and the desired objective of walking away with a small fortune. Also as per a good narrative, these games deliver an emotional charge as we, the viewers, follow the rise and fall of the players' fortunes.

Take It Further: Many motifs can be used as symbols, pointing beyond themselves towards deeper layers of meaning. For instance, the author Tom Chetwynd in his 'Dictionary of Symbols' (Chetwynd, 1982) tells us that a mirror represents the threshold between the conscious and the unconscious or between inner and outer. The moon symbolizes the softer and more soothing light that bonds relationships, and also represents the imagination. Dance represents 'patterns and threads of energy' which bring order out of chaos, on both the cosmic and the personal level.

Note that Chetwynd's interpretation of symbols leans heavily towards the ideas of the psychiatrist Carl Jung. Other sources have it that a mirror symbolizes the reflection of truth (an idea to ponder over); the moon represents the rhythm of time, while dance can symbolize joy but also possession by a 'higher power' either good or evil. Chetwynd's 'Dictionary of Symbols' is the middle volume in a trilogy, the other two books being his 'Dictionary for Dreamers' and 'A Dictionary of Sacred Myth', all three forming his 'language of the unconscious' series.

Note also that symbols are not the same as signs. As we've said, a symbol 'points beyond itself' towards greater or deeper meanings. A sign on the other hand is an image that communicates directly and often serves an immediately practical function. For instance, the sign featuring a black zig-zag within a yellow triangle immediately warns us of danger from electricity – we're warned at a glance. Used as a symbol, lightning can represent the power of the gods (Zeus for instance) or, according to Chetwynd, sudden flashes of insight or intuition that bring ideas from the darkness of the unconscious into the light of conscious thinking as a flash of understanding.

Looking at symbols helps the development of children's metaphorical thinking and heightens their awareness of the difference between literal and figurative language. This in turn can deepen their appreciation of symbolism in literature and film. Also, it can add depth and richness to their own and their classmates' creative writing.

Activities: Colour symbolism is a useful way to begin exploring symbols, as even quite young children will already understand the links between certain colours and emotions and/or other concepts. Split the class into small groups, give each group a colour and ask the children to research its associations before feeding back what they've found to the class.

Look at some pictures of characters from famous children's films (Snow White, Cinderella, Frozen, etc.) and the colours of the clothes the characters wear and how that conveys information about them. There is also an opportunity here to discuss examples of the 'colour stereotypes' that portray the hero in white and the villain in black.

Another activity is to have 'mini discussions' about how some motifs found in stories can have symbolic value. So in SF, for example, a spaceship can represent humankind's 'outward urge' to explore, technological progress or the conquering of the unknown. In horror fiction, a vampire can symbolize immortality, the absence of moral values, loneliness, otherness and basic instincts (or perhaps base instincts). Tom Chetwynd informs us that the vampire represents 'repressed unconscious content which is manifesting destructively'. However, the vampire subgenre has evolved considerably since Bram Stoker's 'Dracula' was published in 1897 and the notion of 'the vampire' is surrounded now by a much richer cloud of associations.

Characters

The word character comes originally from the Greek for 'a stamping tool', something that leaves a distinctive mark. This gives rise to the more familiar sense of a character having distinguishing features.

Characters are obviously primary aspects of narrative, both in fiction and non-fiction – think of science documentaries for example and the way that well-known presenters popularise scientific ideas. Similarly, strong characters make fictional stories more vivid and powerful. As such, as part of the process of creative writing, children should devote some time to thinking about their main characters. Here are some tips and techniques for achieving that –

Activity: Ask children to think of one or two main characters in a favourite story. How has the author managed to create strong, memorable characters (both heroes and villains)? Often we warm to a hero because we identify in some way with him or her. Is that true in this case? Why do we take a hero 'into our hearts'?

Activity: Jigsaw puzzle characters. Fictional characters are often 'composites', with aspects of different people's personalities being brought together to create a new persona. As an experiment, ask young writers to think about people they know – in real life, from TV, books, etc. – and put together a character using different personality traits. (Incidentally, the word persona comes from Latin and refers literally to the mask worn by an actor in a drama.)

Activity: What would XX do? Ask the children to think of a fictional character they like. Then instruct them to write down a situation on a scrap of paper. Situations can be funny, threatening, scary, enjoyable, etc. and need not relate to any situations from the story in which the character appears. Children then swap situations and think about how *their* chosen character would react and why.

Activity: Grab bag of character traits. Explain the idea of character traits to the class; the word 'trait' comes from the Latin meaning a drawing. An early sense of the word was 'the stroke of a pencil on a picture', giving rise to the sense of trait being a particular feature of a drawn character. Help the children to create a list of traits/personal qualities, both positive and negative. Write out each trait on a scrap of paper. Put the scraps in an envelope and draw out three or four each time. Ask children if the selection of traits fits any of the situations they've previously thought of or, if not, what situations would they fit? For example, what situations might require courage, willingness to take chances, selflessness and the ability to make sound judgements? Take the activity further by asking children (if they're prepared to do this) to think of situations from their own lives, and what aspects of their own personality proved to be significant on those occasions. Children can keep their reflections entirely private if they wish.

Character profile. This template, Figure 1.8, might help children to organise their thoughts when developing characters for their stories.

Activity: You can introduce the random factor by asking children to use a polyhedral die. Roll for each chosen characteristic and append the resulting number to those traits. Or, for each dice roll, decide which trait the resulting number would fit. This dampens the tendency for children to make their characters super-strong, super-clever, etc. Take the activity further by thinking of situations where the character's randomly chosen traits would be an advantage and a disadvantage. Using randomly created characters in a story is a useful way of helping to ensure logical consistency in the narrative. So a character who's mild mannered (low

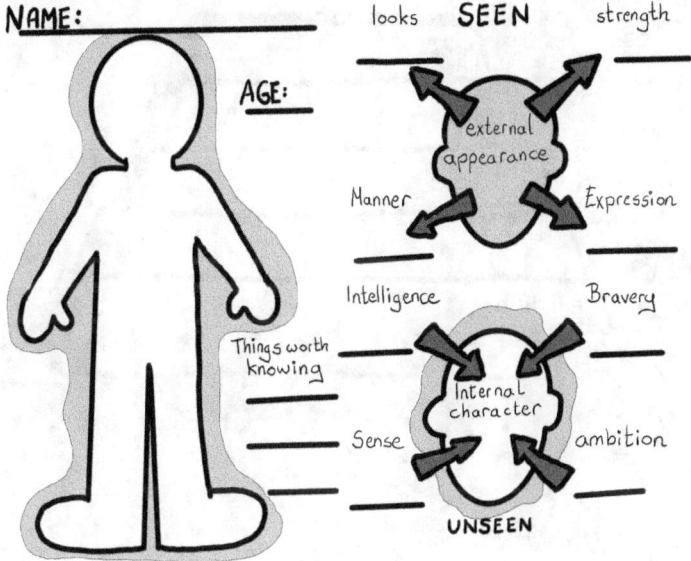

Figure 1.8 Character Profile.

score) would need to be so throughout the story, or would only be loutish or rude for a good reason that fits with the plot, or unless a situation caused the character to be more assertive.

Character pyramid. Similarly, the pyramid template, as shown in Figure 1.9, highlights the fact that main characters at least have depth – the children's author Alan Garner has said that people are like onions; they have layers. A benefit of both the profile and pyramid templates is that they limit the amount of writing children can do. This means that children can be encouraged to give some thought to which details they choose to note, which is important because, especially in short stories, a few vivid details are preferable to long-winded character descriptions, which slow the pace of the story.

Character types. Main characters in particular often evolve over the course of a novel or a sequence of short stories (as they continue on their 'journey'), this fact mirroring what happens in real life – we grow and change through the years. Character types as we're defining the term is the opposite of a stereotype, which is a fixed and generalised form, a kind of off-the-peg cliché in fiction (note that stereotyping actual people or groups is an insidious thing to do, as we look at on page 108). If children are tempted to use off-the-peg characters in their work, encourage them to make at least a couple of changes to the stereotype so that the character is invested with a little freshness or originality.

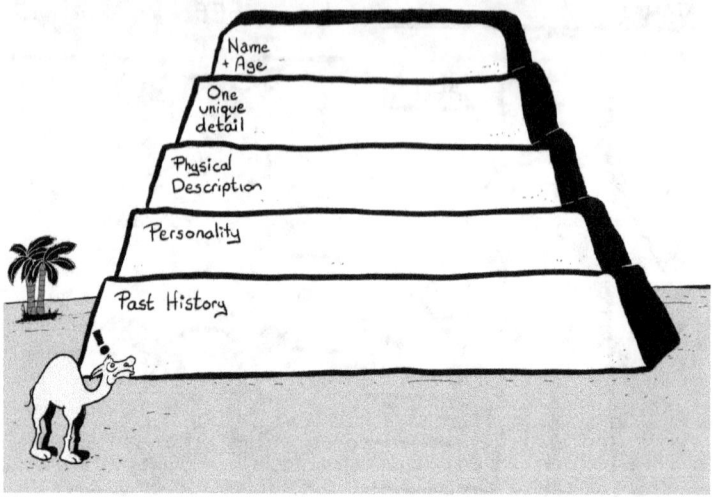

Figure 1.9 Character Pyramid.

Steve – I've used two character types in a range of stories, Ellie and Ben. Ellie first emerged as a 13-year-old, though in more recent stories, she's in her late teens. She's tall, quite thin, blonde, rather shy and self-doubting but has inner strength, which she comes to realise in a crisis. My other character type is Ben. He's usually younger than Ellie (around 11–12) and has straight black hair. He's rather introverted and deep-thinking (what you might call a nerd or geek). He's very intelligent and has extensive knowledge across a narrow range of subjects, mostly relating to the sciences. He loathes sports. Sometimes he appears as Ellie's brother.

Clearly, children can't be asked to create their own character types on the spur of the moment. However, the story profile and pyramid templates serve as a useful start in developing character types over a number of stories. Encourage children to think about this, pointing out that then they won't need to think of new main characters for each story.

Vivid particularities. This is a phrase or sentence that contains at least one vivid descriptive detail and makes an emotional impact. For instance, Steve once taught a girl who had put a purple streak in her hair. She resisted attempts from the Head of Year 'to get rid of it', confiding in Steve that it represented her individuality. Her determination and defiance underpinning the purple streak is a good example of what we're calling a vivid particularity. The technique can be used for people and places, and when used effectively, the reader feels she knows that person or place, conjuring up many more details in the imagination.

Narrative Fiction 27

Figure 1.10 Vivid Particularities.

Activity: The women in Figure 1.10 are about the same age. Ask the children to choose one of the characters and say what one thing differentiates that woman from the others. This could lead to a discussion about what aspects of each of the women engage the attention (expression? posture? clothes?) and make them stand out. Do these details give some indication of their character or attitude? This could then be linked to how an author can often summon up a mental picture in the reader of their characters by using one salient feature rather than lengthier description. Three of the women are carrying what we might call 'props' (a briefcase, a clipboard and a candle) how does that affect how we 'read' their situation: in other words, what can we infer about their lives from these objects?

A Medley of Character-building Activities: Character cards. Use copyright-free images of people as the basis for character making. Stick images on to a card with space for children to write. Their ideas can include a straightforward description without subjective impressions, or subjective impressions such as 'I wouldn't trust him' 'She looks really clever', etc. Write horoscopes for the card characters. Create a timeline from a character's babyhood to the stage they've reached in their life now. Pick out three or four cards at random and imagine that these characters have been brought together somehow. Ask children to speculate on how this might have occurred, how the characters might relate to each other and what could happen next.

Ask children to pick a few of these characters and think about what associations come to mind. Follow up by separating out, where these exist, speculation, opinion and inference. Speculation is a conclusion reached in the absence of evidence or with minimal evidence while an inference is a conclusion based on stronger evidence and on reasoning.

'Narrative Heads'. It's difficult not to make assumptions about people we don't know. Show the children the characters in Figure 1.11. What thoughts do the children have about the characters' personalities? Can the children speculate about any of these people's lives more

28 *Narrative Fiction*

Figure 1.11 Narrative Heads.

generally? Speculations about the characters amount to 'narrative fragments' pointing towards larger and more complex life stories. Note also that there are no right answers to this exercise; each character can be 'read' in a number of ways.

Character boxes. Collect some boxes (shoe box size is ideal). Ask children to bring in several small items and put one or two in each box. Split the class into small groups, give each group a box and ask the children to make inferences about the character who 'owns' the items. Take the activity further by working with one or more other classes. Swap boxes so that your children aren't influenced by any items they've brought in.

Character sketch. Use any of the characters that have been created earlier. Now ask each child in the class to write down a question. Assign a character to a small group, who then sift through a batch of questions and construct responses based on their impressions of the character and the information that comes with the image. Responses can be about any aspect of the character including their strengths, weaknesses, desires, habits, quirks or interests.

The world inside. Split the class into small groups. Ask each group to draw a circle on a large piece of paper – A3 at least or, even better, flip chart or sugar paper. Tell the children that the inside of the circle represents a character's thoughts and feelings. Split the class into small groups. Ask each group to fill the circle with any drawings they care to make, pictures from magazines, abstract shapes and so on. Emphasise that whatever they put into the circle is what's currently on that character's mind. Point out that items in the circle can be metaphorical as well as literal – a car for instance might represent the character's desire to travel or 'get away from it all'. Ask the groups to discuss why their character might be thinking of these things. Once groups have gathered up some ideas, ask them to swap with another group, who repeat the activity for their new character. The groups then pair up and discuss the similarities and differences between their insights.

Gathering Treasures. One way of helping children to become more familiar with thinking metaphorically in this context is to take an object, note some of its characteristics and then apply them to a person. Before going ahead, point out that a 'treasure' is anything precious, so this could be a physical characteristic such as muscular strength or an aspect of the personality such as kindness.

As an example, let's choose a castle. We can easily identify that as being imposing, solid, strong, protective, dependable, standing proud, commanding a good view (far seeing), having control over what to let in and what to let out – what to accept or reject. No doubt children can brainstorm other features. Once a list of characteristics has been created, you can ask what a person would be like who embodied some or all of these features.

Tip: Either pick a character created by an earlier activity or build the beginnings of one by flipping a two-colour counter to get a yes-or-no response to a series of closed questions – Is this person an adult? Is this person a female? The only rules for this simplified version of the game are that questions must be sensible, not frivolous or silly, and cannot contradict previous answers. So if we learn that the character is an adult, then a subsequent question asking if the character is a child must be disallowed. (Note that the counter-flip game is more sophisticated than this and is more fully explained in 'Visualising Literacy and How to Teach It' (Bowkett & Hitchman, 2022).)

Take It Further: Laminate a picture of a castle once the list of characteristics has been generated, place it on the floor, then ask for a volunteer to step onto the laminate and *feel* what it's like to have those characteristics. Impressions can be subjective, so 'It feels nice' or using body language such as standing up straighter are acceptable responses. See also the 'whole class circle' activity on page 136.

This imaginative 'stepping in' technique is a valuable skill in writing creative fiction and in developing a deeper appreciation of stories one reads. Once volunteers have responded to objects, laminate pictures of characters the children have created and repeat the activity. (Again, for more on imaginative stepping-in, see Bowkett & Hitchman, 2022).

Add-a-bit. Children can work individually on this, in pairs or in small groups. Give out a sheet of paper to each child/pair/group. Ask the children to write a small detail or two about a character at the top of the sheet, such as 'Sara is eleven years old and has long dark hair'. Ideally, the details won't be based on characters created in previous activities. Children now pass the sheets around, each time adding a further detail, in this case about Sara's hair. These further details don't need to be purely descriptive but can refer to Sara's life more broadly. So – Sara likes to wear her hair straight. She washes it every other day. She prefers coconut-scented shampoo. Her favourite hair clip is made of silver. The clip was a birthday present from her older brother. Sara would like to put a purple streak in her hair but her mother says no. Sara and Mum argue about this now and then ...

Note that this activity can be used to build settings too.

Just enough. If you've worked through some or all of these character-building activities, the class should have plenty of characters with lots of details attached to them. A useful writing tip at the planning stage is to create more details about people and places than you intend to put in the work. In other words, authors generally know more about their created worlds than they include in their stories.

Activity: Ask children now, working in pairs or small groups, to select a character: If they were going to use that character in a story, what small number of details would they use and why? These can be descriptive details – see the note on 'vivid particularities' on page 26 – or relate to events and situations that characters find themselves in. The activity can also be applied to locations.

Names of People and Places

People's names carry connotations – implied or suggested meanings. Thinking back to Steve's character types (page 25), he feels that Ellie is a 'light and friendly' name, partly because Ellie herself in the stories prefers to be called that rather than the more serious Eleanor, and definitely not Nell or Nellie, which sound too childish to her. Ben is a strong, no-nonsense name. It might not fit that character's persona at age ten or so, but carries the potential to become more appropriate as future events test and develop Ben's inner resources.

Activity: Show the class a list of names (preferably not any of your children's names) and ask if any of the names carry connotations for them. There aren't necessarily any right answers to this activity; the children's ideas can be purely subjective. This is also an opportunity to explore names from different cultures. If children struggle with this activity, offer them a list of adjectives that *you* think can apply to the names. Explain to the class also that names come in and out of fashion. Checking online will show which the most popular names are in different years.

Activity: Ask children to research the origins of names (not necessarily their own). Stephen for instance derives from Greek for wreath or crown, and by extension reward, honour, renown and fame (just as it should be!). Tony or Anthony is an ancient Roman family name, which in turn derives from the Greek name Anteon, son of Hercules (which delights Tony as he's a big fan of Hercules movies).

Nameplay

The essence of any kind of creativity is the preparedness to play with ideas, coupled with a tolerance of ambiguity and uncertainty; of resisting the need to know a right answer right now. This cluster of activities fosters creative wordplay around names, and is particularly applicable to character names for Fantasy, Science Fiction and, to a lesser extent, Horror fiction.

Activity: Take a name such as Brian then subtract one letter to see what happens; Brin, Bran, Rian, Bria. Think about alternative spellings; Brya, Brean, Bryann, Bryanne, Bryen. As a complementary exercise, check the origin of the name – Brian is a Celtic name whose origin is obscure, though it may have links with 'hill' and 'strength'. This might offer further insight into what a character so named (or with a variation) might be like.

Add or scramble letters to the variations that have been created; Abrin, Brant, Briana, Brial, Brylann, Bryannen, Ibryen. Ask children if these carry any connotations for them: to us Bryannen sounds Welsh, for instance. Incidentally, checking baby name websites can throw up real names to add to your lists. We quickly found; Bryannin, Bryannon, Bryannyn and others.

Take It Further: Use a longer word that has potential to be scrambled in many ways. We've chosen 'unafraid'. Figure 1.12 shows how it can be played with –

Fragments	Reverse Fragments	Combi-	-nations
Una	Arfan	Duna	Araf
Nafra	Anu	Danu	Urad
Frai	Diar	Finua	Aruda
Unaf	Arf	Fria	Iana
Afrai	Arfa	Nauf	Daria

Figure 1.12 Playing with Unafraid.

Note that with any activity of this kind, some ideas will work and others won't, in accordance with one of the principles of creativity, which says that to have our best ideas, we need to have lots of ideas.

Another technique is to look in books of myths, legends and folklore, especially ones that are more obscure. Here you will find names that sound authentic but which relatively few people will know, and which therefore will have few or no associations attached to them. Trawling through some reference books threw up; Aodh, Assipattle, Bwbachod, Fuath, Killmoulis, Mooinjer, Yarthkins. Also Audrien, Coraniads, Eladu, Gabhra, Locris, Mesroda, Rath Luachar, Thethra Vran. And Cia-nos, Do-ne-da-do, Gan-nos-gwah, Ho-dar-da-se-do-gas, Quanos (and of course there's nothing stopping children running nameplay activities on these to generate even more variations).

Place Names

Settings and locations are an important aspect of narrative fiction. Some of the same 'rules' that apply to developing characters also relate to settings. Especially in short stories, both characters and settings need to be introduced vividly and economically, with further details added if necessary as the story unfolds and the characters move through their world. Pointing this out to children creates the opportunity to introduce or revisit 'vivid particularities' (page 26) in the form of strong adjectives and verbs, and also the names of particular places. We have not suggested including adverbs at this stage as one tip for more effective writing is to use them sparingly: if they're included in too many activities, children might get into the habit – or find it harder to get out of the habit – of overusing them.

Activities: Ask children to research the name of the town, village or city where they live, or a place they have visited. For instance, Steve grew up in the South Wales mining village of Tylorstown. Its Welsh name is Pendyrus, which according to pendyrus.org (accessed December 2021) could be an amalgamation of 'pen' meaning a peak or a ridge and 'dyrus', which refers to dry and rocky terrain that cannot easily be cultivated (which suits the geography of the area well). Tony's childhood was spent in Leicester. The lineage of that name begins in Anglo-Saxon times, deriving from the Old English element 'caester', which means 'a Roman town'. Long before the Anglo-Saxons, however, when the Romans established the place we now know as Leicester they called it Ratae Corieltauvorum; Ratae being linked to the Latin for 'ramparts', while Corieltauvorum refers to the local Celtic tribe whose capital it served as under the Romans.

Take It Further: For children who find themselves interested in place name origins, much information can be found online, but we would

Narrative Fiction   33

	breck	coomb	grave	holt	lea	mere	rick	slade	scough	tor
autumn										
cloud										
dawn										
fox										
hawk										
moon										
mouse										
raven										
river										
storm										

Figure 1.13 Place Name Generator.

also recommend 'The Concise Oxford Dictionary of Place-names' (Ekwall, 1981). Here you'll find thousands of references. Children may find the book difficult to 'navigate' with its many abbreviated references, so might need adult help.

A much simpler activity is to explain the origins of certain landscape features and then ask them to name-play using the grid in Figure 1.13. So we have –

Breck – a brook
Comb – a valley
Grave – pit
Holt – wood
Lea – forest
Mere – pool
Rick – ridge
Slade – slate
Scough – wood
Tor – rocky peak

Activity: This quick brainstorming activity asks children to offer any associations they have in mind with locations and features of the landscape. So for instance if you say 'woodland', children might come back with spooky, picnic, undergrowth, springtime, earthy smell, fallen leaves, copse, oak (and other trees), shrubbery, grove, clearing and so on. This builds up a bank of vocabulary that children can use subsequently in their writing. It also highlights the power of association and the fact that people's imaginations will throw up different images, thereby leading them to associate, in this case a woodland, in different ways. Extend the activity by giving the class a sentence such as 'The boy was walking through the woods', then ask the children to notice further details in their imagination and write a short description of the boy. Ask children to tell the class what they've written and note how different the descriptions can be.

Activity: Now present the class with one-liners that suggest a location, weather conditions, etc. Ask the children to notice what other details come to mind. So for instance, although 'It was a dark and stormy night' is a cliché, it is probably rich in associations for many children, who might suggest thunder and lightning, 'howling' winds, trees thrashing, leaves blowing, perhaps rainswept streets and so on. This visualisation activity helps children to develop their metacognitive abilities; the facility of noticing and manipulating one's own thoughts.

Activity: Ask the children if they can recall any examples from books, films, comics, where the location was an essential component of the story, and why.

Combi-town

In the same way that authors evolve characters through a series of stories, so some use the same or similar locations multiple times. One example is horror writer Stephen King's Castle Rock, a fictional town in Maine which King uses in a number of his novels, novellas and short stories. What we're calling 'combi-town' is the geographical analogue of the character type (page 25), a location that is fictional but in many cases based on an author's experience and knowledge of actual places. Steve for instance often uses an invented setting called Kenniston. This includes features from his South Wales childhood plus the Midlands town where he lived for some years as an adult. The benefit for children of using a real-but-fictional setting is that they can bring plenty of details easily to mind, but also build in other geographical features necessary for the plot.

Activity: Ask small groups of children to create a location – town, landscape, etc. based on places they know. This might take the form of brief written descriptions and/or a drawn map. Street map templates are easily accessed online if preferred. The activity encourages plenty of conversation and can form the basis for storylines developed in groups or individually.

Drives and Motivations

In the same way that what features in a story must be there for a good reason, so characters must act consistently in line with their drives and motivations.

We made the point earlier that what happens in a story must be there for a reason that's consistent with the internal logic of the narrative. This makes the story more believable or at least, in Fantasy and other genres, makes it easier for readers/viewers to 'suspend disbelief' (a phrase supposedly coined by Samuel Taylor Coleridge in 1817); a willingness to 'buy into' the world of the story.

When you ask children to write a story, it's worth reminding them about the motivations of the characters, and ask them to do a check that the characters do things for believable reasons at the reviewing/revising state.

Emotions

The word motivate is linked to emotion, from the Latin 'move'. Emotions are what move us to act in certain ways. Effective narrative fiction evokes emotions in us, while one aim of developing children's own creative writing is to convey characters' emotions powerfully to the reader.

Activity: Ask children if they can think of a scene from a story that has moved them emotionally in some way (for instance, Steve feels a wave of sadness whenever he recalls Bambi's mother being shot and killed in the Walt Disney film).

Activity: Pick an emotion and ask children to suggest situations where it's likely to be evoked. These can be real-life situations or scenes children remember from stories. (Lists of human emotions are readily available online.)

Activity: Emotion collage. Split the class into small groups and give each group a large sheet of paper. Ask the groups to pick an emotion and create a display using pictures, associated words and colours, abstract shapes and sentences taken from stories or created by the children themselves.

Activity: Ask children working in pairs or small groups to draw a horizontal line on a large sheet of paper. Either give each group a list of five or six emotions, or have children choose for themselves. Tell the groups to spread the emotions along the storyline, as in Figure 1.14, and discuss what situations in a yet-to-be-created story could evoke the feelings in that order. Children may wish to 'lens' their ideas through a chosen

36 Narrative Fiction

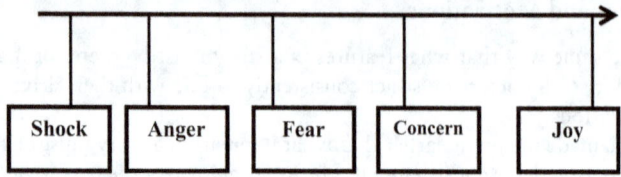

Figure 1.14 Emotions and Storylines.

genre. A variation of the activity is to show the class a storyline-with-emotions and ask groups to create a plot that fits.

Characters as Guides

The children's science fiction writer, the late Douglas Hill, was once asked during a school visit if he felt lonely sitting by himself at home writing his stories. He said, 'No, because I've got so many of my friends with me'. He meant of course the characters that featured in his books. And indeed, favourite characters are like friends; we can feel a sense of warmth towards them and even perhaps a slight sadness when we come to the end of their story – but also excitement and anticipation at reading that story again, or its sequels if further adventures follow.

A more subtle point here relates to the author's 'voice', which in turn is tied in with the author's writing style.

Steve – For me, four authors with a very distinctive voice are the SF writer and visionary Arthur C. Clarke, Ian Fleming through his sequence of James Bond books, the archaeologist Francis Pryor and the philosopher and writer on paranormal topics Colin Wilson. This partly relates to the writing style. When I (re)read their work, I can hear their voices in my head and have a sense of them accompanying me along the way, almost as though they were sitting with me, guiding me through the book. Such 'imaginative hearing' is helped by having watched online clips of these authors lecturing or being interviewed.

Tony – As any parent who has had to constantly read and re-read a favourite story or watch a film that their child seems to love will attest, it is sometimes difficult to put your finger on what it is your child responds to. Similarly, many a parent has read their son or daughter a cherished book from their own childhood only to find it bores them! There is often a gap between what parents, teachers and librarians feel children *ought* to be reading and what they actually like reading. 'Twas ever thus.

Characters and authors we love add to our 'inner resources' that can powerfully affect how we behave and how we feel about ourselves. In this context, we'll come back to the idea in 'Therapeutic Stories'. But for now –

Activity: Ask children to think about fictional characters they love or are affected by in some positive way and why. Discuss how the authors manage to create characters that have such a powerful effect on our emotions. Have any children changed how they think, feel and behave because of the influence of a fictional character?

Person

You've probably already taught your children about first, second and third person – the I-voice, the you-voice and the he-she or it voice. Writing in the first person draws us into a character's mind and lets us see the world as that individual perceives it. The disadvantage of using first person is that we are 'stuck' with that character and have to go wherever he (or she or it) goes. Writing in the second person means that the author is talking directly to the reader, so creating a feeling of directness and immediacy. The most well-known use of second person in fiction is in the many choose-your-own adventure books that first appeared in the early 1980s and that are still popular today. Writing in the third person allows the author to move about in time and space in the world of the story and so makes for a very versatile way of telling a tale. Most stories we've encountered are written in the third person.

Activity: An effective way of familiarising children with the concept of person, once you've explained it, is to present them with some extracts and ask them to rewrite in a different person; from first to third, first to second, etc.

Activity: It's not easy to plan a choose-your-own-adventure (CYOA) (we know because we've tried), but if you want the children to have a go, split the class into small groups and give each group a copy of a CYOA book and a stock of blank postcards or scraps of paper. They can base their adventure on stories of their own, or plots from other books – though their CYOAs will be very brief. Once children have written their story opener on a postcard or paper scrap (in the second person), get them to number the scrap as 1, then think of two alternative scenarios that arise from it ... 'You are walking through the woods alone when you hear the roar of some monstrous creature coming closer. Do you run (go to 2) or hide (go to 3)?'

Obviously, each alternative has two further scenarios arising from it, so a CYOA becomes complex very quickly. Children are free to think up their own scenarios of course, but they should include at least one where the main character dies and at least one where he or she survives and makes it to the end. Using blank postcards or paper scraps means that children can physically arrange and rearrange them on the tabletop, alter or discard them as necessary, and see the whole story-so-far at a glance.

Finally, we'll mention that writing in the third person creates a 'psychologically distant' vantage point, an idea we'll revisit in 'Therapeutic Stories'.

Fictional Genres

As we saw earlier (page 15), the word genre comes from early 19th-century French and means literally 'a kind'. There is also a link with 'gender', deriving originally from Latin meaning 'kind, sort, genus'. In talking about fictional genres, we mean Fantasy, Science Fiction, Horror, Romance, Thriller, Mystery, Spy, Westerns, Pirates, Crime, Historical. Comedy and Adventure are sometimes included in a list of fictional genres, although these can also be thought of as story 'ingredients' (see page 15), that help to flavour and colour a story – so we could consider comedy Horror for example as being a subgenre of Horror.

(Note that the difference between a thriller and a mystery is that in a thriller, the author attempts to create a sense of dread or nervous anticipation about a future crime, while in a mystery, the reader is aware of the crime or wrongdoing, but the story focuses on the protagonist tracking the villain down, to be revealed towards the end. Note too that the term 'genre' is also applied to what we prefer to think of as different *forms* of writing; descriptive, expository, journals and letters, narrative, persuasive and poetry (according to the aresearchguide.com, accessed December 2021).

Discussing genre with the class allows children to revisit the notions of motifs and conventions, these being expressed through all aspects of the story; themes, characters, events, objects and other motifs.

Activity: Split the class into small groups. Either allocate each group a genre or allow children to choose for themselves from genres they are familiar with. Instruct them to pick a story from their chosen genre and list the themes, characters, etc. they find there then share their ideas with the class.

Activity: Ask the groups to create a display that captures the essence of their chosen genres using images, extracts from stories and poems, the children's own drawings and even small objects that can be fixed to the display board.

Activity: Have children devise some titles for stories from their chosen genre. A simple way of doing this is to collect titles of already existing stories and cherry pick from them to create new titles. Referring again to the author Douglas Hill (page 36), some of Doug's titles are; Blade of the Poisoner, The Huntsman, The Dragon Charmer, Warriors of the

Wasteland, Master of Fiends, Creatures of the Claw, Deathwing Over Veynaa and Planet of the Warlord. Even if some children aren't interested in SF or Fantasy, they can still play around with the titles above to come up with new combinations – Dragons of the Wasteland, Blade of the Huntsman, The Dragon Poisoner, Creatures of the Warlord, for instance. And of course, the more titles children collect, the more combinations they'll be able to create.

Activity: We mentioned earlier that the term genre is sometimes used for what we prefer to think of as different forms of writing. Figure 1.15 makes the distinction clear, with forms on the vertical axis and genres across the top. If you want children to write, plan or at least think about genre fiction, then matching a chosen genre with one or more forms offers greater versatility. So a child could choose to write a science fiction diary, another a fantasy blog, another child might prefer to compose a poem about pirates. Some of the written forms can make use of what we call the 'minimal writing strategy'. Some children shy away from creative writing. We've found that this can be due to a 'failure of imagination', where children think they don't know how to have ideas (we hope that at least some of the activities in this book address the issue!). Sometimes we encounter a 'failure of nerve', where children are nervous about having a go in case they don't 'do well' or are judged negatively against their peers. The solution to this is to establish a 'we're all in it together' ethos in the classroom, a community of writers where we celebrate having a go at tackling different writing challenges. A powerful aspect of a supportive ethos is where the adults in the classroom also do some writing and are prepared also to discuss any difficulties they had. See Steve's 'Developing Self-Confidence in Young Writers' (Bowkett, 2017) for more.

The minimal writing strategy can take many forms. A child could simply think about a story, make notes and write just the opening

	SF	Fantasy	Horror	Spy	Crime	Thriller	Pirate
Story							
Poem							
Blog							
Diary							
Journals							
Script							
Letter							
Essay							
Advert							

Figure 1.15 Form and Genre.

scene or the exciting climax. A poem could take the form of a haiku – not much writing but plenty of thinking involved. Another technique is the minisaga, where children attempt to tell a story in fifty words, or as near as they can get to that. We've also used the counter-flip game (page 29) to encourage children to overcome their writing reluctance. The technique can be used to develop characters, settings, storylines – indeed all three. It usually works well because, while the child is responsible for the questions she asks, there can be no wrong answers; just an accumulation of information that increasingly informs subsequent questions.

Activity: Lensing. One of the key principles of creative thinking is to look at things in different ways. This activity involves children choosing a genre and then combining it with a 'what if' scenario that they or you supply (see also page 138 in the section on 'Stories and Learning'). A 'neutral' picture, such as that shown in Figure 1.16, or locations that children are familiar with serve as a stimulus.

What-ifs could be; what if aliens invaded the Earth? What if vampires really existed? What if you found a dragon's nest and tried to hatch one of the eggs at home? (We revisit what-ifs on page 160.)

As soon as children choose or are presented with a what-if, their view of the picture or location stimulus is now 'lensed' or interpreted through that genre. Without any effort, children begin to imagine aliens invading their home town, or a vampire trying to get into their house or keeping a dragon's egg a secret from their friends. Again, any written outcome could take one of the forms of writing suggested above.

Figure 1.16 Stimulus for Lensing.

Tone, Atmosphere and the Spirit of Place

In 'combi-town' (page 34), we saw how writers can develop a setting and use it over many stories. In the same way that an author can come to consider his characters as friends, so favourite settings can evoke a special feeling; places that a writer looks forward to revisiting. In that sense, settings can have more than a practical value in helping to tell a story.

Many children probably learn tacitly that settings are important aspects of a narrative before they are formally taught this. You can raise their awareness even further in the following ways –

Activity: Think of a favourite story and decide how some of the settings were important in telling the tale.

Activity: Notice how authors introduce a setting in their stories (whether you've read them or not). Here are some examples that we've found –

> 'They reached the end of the alley and saw Jondo duck behind a mass of brambles on the wasteland that separated the town's southern estate from the park and the arboretum or tree garden. Birtles snatched up some stones and threw them on a high curve to take them over the barbed-wire jungles of blackberry runners and nettles behind which Jondo had disappeared.'

Here the author contrasts the pleasant idea of the arboretum and the ugly wasteland with its nettles and brambles, highlighting the difficulty Jondo has running away from the bully Birtles.

> 'Eleanor glanced back through the darkness and saw the glow of the fires and the tiny paper lanterns and the dancing shapes like a pocketful of jewels far, far away. Now the waning moon and autumn stars seemed closer, with torn wisps of cloud like old lace draped above the trees. Small breezes slipped through the branches and plucked down thin scatterings of leaves, the ones that were ready to fall.'

The author wants to contrast the light and cosiness of the outdoor Halloween party with the darkness beyond at this particular time of year.

> 'It was six o'clock and the streets were wet-black, shimmering under light rain and a strong leaf-littered wind. Across the way the park was an ocean of darkness. Along the main street shops were closing up, but bars and coffee houses were still doing good trade and would remain open till late.'

This extract, written by the same author as the previous one, pinpoints the particular time in the evening between day and night – the word evening coming from Old English meaning 'the time between sunset and darkness'; when light and dark are evenly balanced, we presume. Again there's the sense of contrast between the cosiness, busyness and light of the main street and the 'ocean of darkness' beyond, with 'ocean' suggesting something huge, unknown and perhaps dangerous.

> 'I watched with Nige as the little two-carriage train pulled away into the darkness, filling the air with the smell of diesel and steel, which both of us quite liked.'

Here the author is relying on the reader having stood on a railway platform at night – a small stop in the village or town. The mention of the diesel and steel smell adds another sensory dimension, while the use of the first person gives the experience of the place immediacy.

> 'You could smell the apples, sweet and tempting, in the still September air. We were crouched down behind clumps of willow herb overlooking the allotments. The purply-pink flowers had withered and died, and by Christmas the patch would be nothing more than dead sticks …'

This author too uses smell to make the scene more evocative. Mention of the dead willow herb lets us know that the narrator notes the passage of the seasons and is maybe already looking forward to Christmas.

Activity: Think about places you know. Do any of them have a particular feel? That is to say, can you think of any places that bring out certain emotions in you? Can you pinpoint why?

Activity: Ask children to note the techniques the authors above have used to evoke a sense of place, then think of a location and use it to set the scene in a few sentences.

Many people, including writers, artists, musicians and other creatives, celebrate the 'spirit' of a place; the unique, distinctive and cherished aspects of a particular location, a type of landscape and even a country. As children talk about the feelings places bring out in them, you may feel it's appropriate to introduce them to this concept.

Steve – Whenever I visit Leicester Cathedral, I experience a deep sense of comfort and peace. It would be easy to explain this away by saying I'm just associating what I see with the underpinning messages of Christianity (love, kindness, compassion, etc.) but I don't recall having these feelings in other cathedrals or churches. Conversely, there's a 10th-century church not far from where we live that my wife won't enter, telling me that there's 'something bad' about the place that she can't put her finger on.

Twenty Questions

This popular game can be used to help children sharpen up their critical thinking and questioning skills. The activity can also be scaffolded to accommodate different ages and ability levels. We prefer to use a 6 × 6-cell grid, as shown in Figure 1.17, because dice rolls can be used to choose an item at random and also because all of the information featured in the activity is 'visually available' at a glance.

Activity: Have one of the children choose an animal from the grid, telling no one but yourself of the selection – you will need to be available to advise if a child doesn't understand a question or doesn't know the answer. Questions can be asked by individuals or by pairs or small groups who can be given time to discuss their questions in advance. Blind guesses are not allowed: if a child wants to name the chosen animal, he must give his reasoning as well. The primary aim of the game isn't for any child or group to win by finding the correct term first: raising children's awareness of using relevant vocabulary to frame incisive

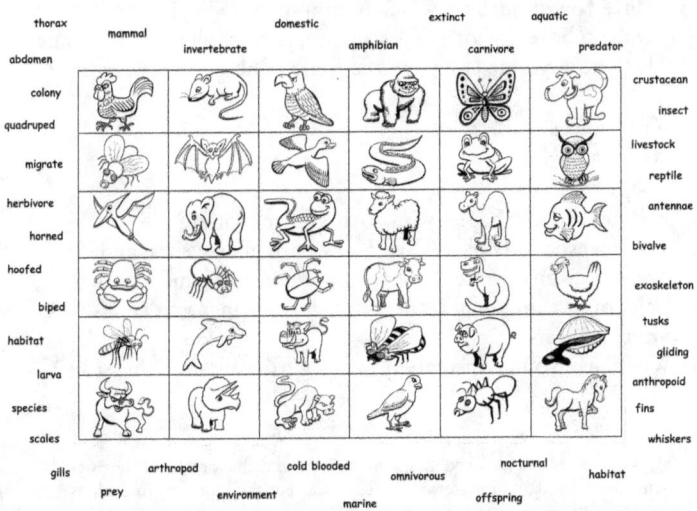

Figure 1.17 Twenty Questions Grid.

questions is the point. As you'll realise, the activity can fit within a range of subject areas.

Children can also create their own 6 × 6 grids based on favourite stories. The grids can be entirely word-based, picture-based or a mixture. Large grids make attractive displays that you can share with other classes. You can also increase the challenge if you run the activity subsequently by allowing only 19 questions, then 18 and so on – though obviously, there will be a limit to the minimum number of questions that can hope to uncover the answer.

Story Checklist

This will be used when children are at the planning stage of writing a story; as a tool for looking back at stories they've completed; or as a way of thinking critically about stories by other writers.

11) Is the story based on at least one theme?
10) Are some or all of the basic narrative elements built into the storyline?
9) Do some motifs/conventions appear in the story to pinpoint its genre?
8) If the story doesn't fall within a genre, how could you describe it?
7) If the idea has been used before, are you bringing anything fresh to it?
6) Have you mapped out a basic storyline?
5) Do you have your characters clearly in mind?
4) Have you thought about the setting(s) in the story?
3) Have you decided on which person to write in (1st, 2nd, 3rd)?
2) Do you have a strong first sentence, paragraph or scene in mind?
1) Is there anything else you need to think about before staring?

Write your story.
Looking back –

1 Are you broadly happy with what you've written?
2 Are you especially pleased with any particular scenes, and if so why?
3 Are you dissatisfied with any parts of the story, and if so why?
4 Can you use anything from the story, or things you've discarded, in future projects?*
5 What have you learned about writing from creating this story?

---

* This is called 'recycling'. We've seen it in the form of themes, character types and 'combitowns', but any part of a story can be reused; punchy sentences and phrases, strong adjectives and verbs, snatches of dialogue, etc. plus ideas considered but discarded at the planning stage. Recycling follows the basic principle in writing that 'nothing is ever wasted'.

Writing Effectively

Here are some generally recognised principles for writing robust and memorable narrative fiction. Trying to explain them all at once might overload some children, so we suggest introducing them one at a time as appropriate to the children's learning.

Keep the writing clear and simple. Don't be tempted to overwrite or use 'clever' words to impress anyone. Although your work may be marked and graded, it's very important that you enjoy your writing, which also means that you'll learn more about the process when you do.

The most enjoyable writing 'flows' on to the page or screen. Although accurate spelling and punctuation are important, don't interrupt your writing to think about them. For example, just write a word you're not sure of as you think it's spelt, and check it and any others later when you look back at your work. Even the most experienced authors go back over their work, sometimes several times, to tidy it up and try to improve it.

Avoid being vague. As you write you'll have pictures of your characters and locations streaming through your mind. Notice the details of these and write just enough so that your readers can create impressions in their imaginations too.

Think about your other senses. As well as pictures you can imagine sounds, textures, smells and tastes. Include these in your writing – though remember, 'just enough'.

Ease off from using too many adjectives and adverbs as these can make the writing look 'cluttered'. Also, using 'said' after speech is fine; there's no need to try and use different verbs every time, like shouted, whispered, grunted, etc. 'Said' is like a punctuation mark that's hardly noticed by the reader. Its job is simply to help readers keep track of who's speaking.

Vary the length of your sentences and paragraphs as this helps to keep the writing fresh. Use shorter sentences in action scenes. Avoid overlong paragraphs and long sequences of dialogue with no description/exposition (explanation).

Note that dialogue in a story isn't the same as when we speak. Notice how people speak – there are pauses, repetitions, changes of tense, contradictions and lots of other 'clutter'. If you tried to include these in dialogue, it would look very messy and your readers would struggle through it.

Show don't tell. This means trying to recreate what your characters are going through in your readers' imaginations. If you say, 'Bowman was terrified' you're telling the reader that he was. To show that Bowman was terrified, you could mention him sweating, his heart pounding, his limbs trembling, etc.

If you're writing in the third person, don't jump from one character's point of view to another's in the same scene – this is called 'head hopping'. Stick with the same character's point of view for the whole scene, switching to another character in the next scene if you need to.

Remember that your characters will look at the world in their own way, which will be different for each character. A confident character will not see the world in the same way as a nervous and anxious character for example. Thinking about your characters before you write helps you to describe the world as they see it. Technically this is called a 'character filter'.

Give more 'page time' to your main characters. Minor characters can be mentioned in passing and you don't usually need to tag them with much descriptive detail.

Avoid melodrama. This is where exaggerations are used to make a scene over-dramatic. In our 'show don't tell' advice, we used the example of Bowman being terrified. Terror is an extreme emotion and so something truly awful must have happened to make Bowman feel that way. Think about what emotions your characters would be likely to experience in any given situation.

Use 'active' language rather than 'passive' language as far as possible – technically this is called 'voice'; the active and the passive voice. Writing 'The card was sent by Bowman' is passive, while 'Bowman sent the card' is active; something he actively did. Using the active voice makes your writing more dynamic.

Above all, as we've advised, enjoy your writing.

Steve – Some years ago I wrote stories about a group of friends called the Double Darers, who used to dare each other to do things (see page 141). But they have a motto that they always honour, which is; 'Dare to do it and do your best. Have fun, but hurt no one'. The same can be said of our writing.

* * *

2   Myths, Legends, Fairy Tales and Folklore

The word myth derives from the Greek *muthos* meaning 'narrative speech'. Today the term is often taken to refer to something that's not true, or that is 'just' the product of the imagination, but one of the main purposes of this section is to explore the idea that myths and 'mythic fragments' (short narratives that point to a greater narrative landscape) are built deeply into the human psyche and can act as important templates in shaping our morality, our decisions and our behaviours. Further, myths and legends have existed for thousands of years. In his book 'Flag Fen: life and death of a prehistoric landscape' (Pryor, 2015) archaeologist Francis Pryor asserts that the local landscape – and presumably other landscapes across the globe – was far less important than the map people carried in their heads. 'This map would have been peopled by stories, myths and legends and it would also have been shaped by the deeds, real and imaginary, of the individual's own relatives and ancestors. In short it was a landscape of the mind...'

In his contributory essay 'The Necessity of Myth', which appears in 'Myth and Mythmaking', edited by Henry A. Murray (Murray, 1968), American writer and critic Mark Schorer advises that the definition of myth must be both broad and loose, as myth operates both universally and diversely; i.e. across all cultures in very different ways. Similarly, in his book 'The Universal Myths: heroes, gods, tricksters and others', American writer Alexander Eliot (Eliot, 1990) cautions that myth eludes definition, while in his companion volume 'The Timeless Myths: how ancient legends influence the modern world' (Eliot, 1997), he suggests that with regard to myths, 'Think then not of true or false, but whether myths evoke a meaningful response ... whether they are adequate or inadequate'. This resonates with the idea we mention elsewhere (page 6) that a simplistic separation of fact and fiction is misleading: stories can 'tell us something true', while facts (ideas manufactured by humans) are provisional and liable to change. We'll touch on this later in the section on narratives in science. Also arising from Eliot's comment is the implication that a 'meaningful response' will in many, if not most, cases be created by the individual. The early Doctor Who stories have a mythic quality for Steve: it would be interesting if the 'new Who' (the programme was revived in 2005 after being off the air for 16 years) has a deeper meaning for today's young viewers – You can ask them of course!

Activity: Ask children if any modern stories have helped them to live happier and more fulfilling lives, or at least if they have positively influenced the way they feel. Have any modern stories taught them anything about the best way to behave and get on with people? Are any characters from stories role models in other ways?

Activity: The subtitle of Eliot's 'The Timeless Myths' implies no difference between a myth and a legend. Ask children to research any differences and share their findings, or supply them with distinctions you've discovered and discuss these with the class.

According to the edb.gov.hk website (accessed December 2021), a myth is a traditional story that explains what people within their culture believe about the natural and human world: the Navajo story of Coyote and the Black God explains why some stars are brighter than others; the myth of Persephone explains the seasons; the torment of Loki explains earthquakes; while creation myths explain how and why we are here, including how the universe came about – the Orphic creation myth of Ancient Greece for instance posits the 'hatching' of all there is from a Cosmic Egg. Myths may be individual stories with characters and a narrative but they are fundamentally a part of a belief system, albeit one that no one may subscribe to any longer. The main characters in myths are usually gods or supernatural heroes and the stories are set in the distant past. The people who told these stories believed that they were true.

A legend is a traditional story about the past. The main characters are usually kings or heroes. Some examples of well-known legends include the tales of Odysseus from Ancient Greece, Beowulf from the Norse lands and King Arthur from Old England. Like myths, legends may have been thought to be true. A legend is built around an event or person, often from a specific period – the Trojan War for instance may have happened, but certainly not like in the legends; it is the peg on which to hang the stories of Achilles, the Wooden Horse and numerous other tales. Billy the Kid did exist but dime novels, comics and films fabricate countless fictional narratives around him. With some legends, particularly those based on tales told and retold in the distant past, their source (historical or otherwise) may have been lost. For example, there probably was no historical Robin Hood, but folktales mentioning him from the 12th century onwards may or may not have their origin in the exploits of some contemporary outlaw. Either way Robin Hood stories have kept generations of people enthralled through the years. Legends are fictions spun around a specific character, event or period that may bear little or no resemblance to what (if any) historical record exists.

Activity: Ask children to choose a historical figure such as Robin Hood and do some research to try and find out if he really existed or not.

Activity: We have asserted that stories can 'tell us something true'. Discuss with the class what children think is meant by 'truth' and how things they believe or know to be true can be tested or proved.

Mark Schorer in 'Myths and Mythmaking' sums up these ideas by telling us that myths are instruments by which we continually struggle to make our experience intelligible to ourselves. In that sense, they fulfil one of the primary purposes of narrative by offering a template or pattern for creating a sense of order and sequence in our lives. Schorer calls this a 'controlling image' – insofar as we take control by making sense of our experiences – that gives philosophical meaning (fundamental knowledge) to ordinary life. The American psychologist Rollo May in his 'The Cry for Myth' echoes this view by summarising the value of myths –

Myths contribute to our sense of personal identity by exploring the question 'Who am I?' perhaps because we measure ourselves against the characteristics and behaviours of the dramatis personae of the myths we encounter, especially those we take to heart. The American Yoga teacher Richard Hittleman in his 'Guide to Yoga Meditation' (Hittleman, 1969) devotes a chapter to 'the great riddle of the self'. There he asks readers to try to answer the question 'who am I?' pointing out that many people will come up with a list of labels *about* themselves while failing to touch on the essence of their individuality. This meshes with an idea developed by the Victorian poet Gerard Manley Hopkins. Hopkins felt that each created thing had its own uniqueness, which he called a being's 'inscape'. Expressing that uniqueness through life he called 'instress'; what fellow poet Dylan Thomas might well be referring to as 'the force that through the green fuse drives the flower', the vital energy behind one's individuality expressed in life. Many of Hopkins's poems explore this idea very powerfully and beautifully (see for example his 'As kingfishers catch fire, dragonflies draw flame', poem 34 in Gardner, 1970). We feel that it's important for children to become aware of these ideas, as most children and young people are surely striving to establish a sense of identity and, ideally, uniqueness (however much a child wants to fit in with a group).

Activity: Ask children if they would like to *be* any character in stories they know, and why. (They may wish to keep their thoughts to themselves in some cases.)

Tony – Mind you, perhaps not always appealing to our best angels: as a kid I always liked the Hulk, not because of any of his good qualities but because he was big and a strong and green and could smash things! (Steve – He hasn't changed.)

Second, Rollo May feels that myths make possible our sense of community, insofar as they embody shared truths, beliefs and loyalties, as defined earlier. Every culture has its own heritage (that which is inherited), passed on in the form of narratives that range from over-the-fence gossip to scientific/religious/spiritual accounts of how the universe and each of us came into being – for more on this, see 'The Ladder to the Moon' on page 52.

Activity: Ask the children if they can recall any event, perhaps seen on the news, that created for them a sense of community, whether locally, nationally or globally. For us, what immediately springs to mind are the Apollo moon shots (viewed on TV by much of the world's population), the death of Princes Diana in 1997, which united the UK in grief; and more recently stepping outside to clap for National Health Service (NHS) staff and other heroes in the early months of the COVID pandemic, and of course the Queen's 70th Jubilee Weekend and, sadly, Her Majesty's death not long afterwards.

Activity: Discuss the notion of loyalty and affinity with the class. Do children have a favourite actor, pop group, football team, etc.? How do they feel about their country? What do they understand by the idea of community? Do they feel that their school, year or class qualify as a kind of community? Can loyalty have a negative side? If so, what are some examples of this? It hardly needs saying that some children's feelings will run deep when it comes to notions of patriotism, so discussions need to be conducted sensitively.

Steve – I was born and grew up in South Wales. Some years ago I had an acquaintance who was deeply patriotic[*] and who took issue with me for saying that while I enjoyed my Welsh upbringing, I couldn't say that I felt patriotic about Wales, and certainly not in the negative sense of thinking Wales was 'better' than other countries, or of feeling antagonistic about other countries or cultures. I was startled to discover, during the same conversation, that my acquaintance was born in North Wales (three miles from the English border!) and that he was biased against Welsh people living in the south. For me there was something unhealthily divisive about such a view, which could lead to adherence to any number of unfortunate 'isms'.

---

[*] Patriot comes originally from the Greek *patris* meaning 'fatherland', through *patrios*, 'of one's fathers' and then late Latin *patriota*, 'fellow countrymen'.

Rollo May asserts that a third important function of myth is to 'undergird our moral values'. He goes on to express his concern that cultivating a sense of moral value is crucially important nowadays, 'when morality has deteriorated and seems to have vanished altogether in some distraught places'. You may or may not agree with him on that. Our own view is that while the news (another form of narrative) is laden with stories of horror and disaster, countless stories of goodness, kindness and generosity never make national headlines – though some news channels often finish a programme with tales of this kind, to end on an upbeat note.

Activity: You may need to explain that morality is an understanding of good and bad, right and wrong as these apply to our thoughts, feelings and behaviours. We think that discussing morality is best done through a philosophical enquiry. The procedure for setting one up is beyond the scope of this book, but you could try Steve's 'Jumpstart! Philosophy in the Classroom' (Bowkett, 2018) and Jason Buckley's 'Pocket P4C' – philosophy for children – (Buckley, 2011). Also, philosopher Stephen Law has written two books, 'The Philosophy Files' aimed specifically at children. In these, he explores moral issues through chapters such as, 'where do right and wrong come from?', 'killing people' and 'does Murderous Mick deserve to be punished?' Laws' essays are informative and engaging both for children and adults. And if you wanted to delve deeper, you might try Martin Cohen's '101 Ethical Dilemmas' (Cohen, 2004). Incidentally, one of the most interesting distinctions we've come across between morals and ethics is summed up by the aphorism that 'An ethical person knows it's wrong to steal, while a moral person doesn't steal', an idea that is itself ripe for discussion.

The fourth purpose of mythology according to Rollo May is that it is 'our way of dealing with the inscrutable mystery of creation'. Trivialisers of myth say that myths were stories made up by people from prescientific (or even 'primitive') cultures to explain natural phenomena that they didn't previously understand. We find this to be both patronising and misguided, given what the authorities we've quoted have to say about the purpose and value of myths within the human condition. And while, in the modern age, scientific narratives exist about how the universe and life came into existence, that doesn't address the burning issue of *personal* purpose and meaning, which is more properly addressed through the narratives of the Arts, philosophy and religion/spirituality. While creation myths might not be literally true, they can still convey truth, if only that the universe does have meaning and purpose that relates to individual lives – again something ripe for discussion.

The Ladder to the Moon

Imagine a ladder stretching from the Earth to the Moon, with the rungs of the ladder representing different kinds of stories. At the base, we have jokes, anecdotes and 'earthy' tales. Then in ascending order there are; shaggy dog stories (rambling tales ending irrelevantly, sometimes with an atrocious pun), family stories, ancestor tales, folk tales, historical stories, fables, wonder tales (Ref: https://katefarrell.net/wonder-tale/), legends, myths, sacred (holy) stories and origin and creation stories. The symbolic power of the ladder to the moon is that it tells us that all stories are connected, and that everyday gossip is as necessary as overarching narratives that attempt to answer the big existential questions such as; what is reality, what is life, do we have free will, is the universe deterministic and what is consciousness? Again, all three of the great pillars of human enquiry – science, philosophy and religion – address these and other deep issues through their own narratives.

Activity: If you or any of the children have an artistic flair, create a wall display featuring the ladder to the moon, as in Figure 2.1. Mark off the different kinds of stories, then ask children to find examples of stories for each category. Children may want to summarise these tales, draw them, photocopy book covers, panels from comics, etc.

Activity: Remind children of the basic narrative template (page 18). Split the class into small groups and ask them to look at two or three myths to see how closely they map on to the template. Earlier we made the point that popular and successful stories follow the pattern quite closely, as will some well-known and enduring myths.

Activity: What modern stories do the children know about that have the mythic qualities we've been exploring?

Gossip and Rumours

These occupy the same place on the ladder as earthy tales and overlap with them. Adjunct Professor and storyteller Gail de Vos in her book 'Tales, Rumors and Gossip' (de Vos, 1996) draws a distinction between gossip and rumours (the title of her book uses the American spelling). Gossip is defined as idle talk and tittle-tattle, especially about other people and social events. Rumour has been defined as general talk, reports or hearsay of doubtful accuracy, and while rumours may involve specific individuals, they are often concerned with places and events of greater scope and importance.

Myths, Legends, Fairy Tales and Folklore 53

Figure 2.1 Ladder to the Moon.

Steve – Rumours are not always malicious. The best joke played on me by a pupil while I was teaching concerned 'the great cake and biscuit sale'. Notices to be read out in assembly were brought to the secretary's office beforehand and were checked to see that they'd been signed by a teacher. On this particular occasion, one notice in a Year-Seven assembly (I had a Year Nine tutor group so didn't need to be there), supposedly signed by me, announced a 'great cake and biscuit sale' in my classroom that morning break, with all proceeds going to charity. Imagine my surprise when, as break began, dozens of pupils from years seven, eight and nine – and even some staff! – flocked into my room and demanded to know why there were no cakes or biscuits on sale. The rumour had gone round the school in under two hours. I spent all break time explaining what had happened and virtually everyone saw the funny side of it. I never found out who'd forged the note and my signature, but if I had I'd have given that child a merit mark. I didn't get a coffee either!

Activity: Do the children know of any (non-defamatory) rumours circulating in school or around the neighbourhood? Have they ever heard a non-defamatory rumour that they believed, or still believe?
Gail de Vos also notes similarities between gossip, rumours and contemporary legends –

They all use concrete details and dialogue to make the stories more credible and contain 'inside' information that doesn't usually feature good news.
All often focus on unusual events and experiences. These are rooted in or related to the kinds of actual experiences and events relevant to the teller and the listener.
All such accounts evolve and can be updated with recent 'facts' and supposed evidence.
All three forms can serve as teaching tales and cautionary stories on how or how not to behave.

Also in her book, de Vos offers six reasons as to why people spread rumours –

Rumours count as news. Most people perhaps like to have a sense of what's going on in the world, however shaky the story.
People's understanding of events can be clarified by talking about them. Listeners to a rumour can act as a sounding-board to help interpret, strengthen or lessen the teller's belief in the story.
Recounting rumours can reinforce the teller's own views, sometimes with the aim of persuading listeners to believe them too.
Sometimes rumours help to release tensions and anxieties – 'Thank goodness it didn't happen to me!'
Rumours also count as entertainment. People enjoy listening to stories that are surprising, shocking or funny. See also Urban Folktales on page 71, which share these features.
Rumours can help to fuel casual conversation, serving as conversation-fillers or ice breakers; the oil that lubricates the social machine.

Joseph Campbell

Towards the other end of the Ladder to the Moon, we have fables, wonder tales and myths. When George Lucas was developing his epic Star Wars stories, he consulted the well-known mythologist Joseph Campbell with the aim in mind of creating 'a myth for the twentieth century'. Campbell's academic achievements are impressive, including his huge 'The Masks of God' series of volumes and his popular 'The Hero with a Thousand Faces'. Later in his life Campbell discussed the nature of mythology and its relevance to the modern day, his commentaries being published in books such as 'The Power of Myth' in conversation with journalist Bill Moyers (Campbell, 1988) and 'The Way of Myth' in conversation with author, actor and director Fraser Boa (Campbell, 1994).

Campbell expresses some deeply held beliefs about myth. He informs us that mythology as a whole has four important functions (you may want to compare these with Eliot's ideas on pages 57 and 67) –

The mystical/metaphysical function, which is to inculcate us with a sense of awe and gratitude before the 'mystery of being' and our participation in it.
The cosmological function, which explains the nature of the universe.
The sociological function, which is to support and validate the existing social order.
The pedagogical/psychological function, which is to guide the individual through the different stages of life.

Campbell believed that some of the problems facing western/westernised cultures have arisen from the fact that such cultures have become 'demythologised', suffering from a lack of underpinning narratives to cohere the primary functions of myth (a view shared by Rollo May, page 49). He also felt that many young men in such cultures go 'off the rails' or are confused and rudderless in life because they are not formally initiated into adulthood. In his conversation with Fraser Boa, Campbell mentions some of the (to our eyes) brutal initiation rituals inflicted on young men in certain cultures that allow them to step over the threshold from childhood to adulthood. Campbell links this with his observation that girls automatically and naturally become women with their first period; that 'nature does it to them', and that some of the agonising rituals men endure allow them to understand and share the pain that women experience during childbirth. Campbell echoes a comment by the philosopher Friedrich Nietzsche, that 'Man today, stripped of myth, stands famished amongst all his pasts ...' While the psychologist Jerome Bruner (quoted in 'The Cry for Myth') feels that so many people are engaged in a 'lonely search for internal identity', in the absence of myths undergirding their lives.

Activity: The younger children of our target age range are perhaps too young to have direct experience of these concepts, and indeed you may not want to mention them at all. We offer them as a background to Campbell and his work. If any of the children have watched any of the Star Wars movies, ask them if they can recall some of the motifs and conventions (page 15) that help to define the saga as 'a myth for the twentieth century'; a guide offering insights about good and evil and a template for 'right living'.

At many points in his discussion of mythology, Campbell asserts that myths are an expression of 'visual dream images' of the energies that inform the body. We take this to mean that the motifs found in myths are metaphors for the deep thoughts, feelings and behaviours that human beings experience. Not all of these are conscious: there is a certain surreal quality to some myths (and legends and fairy tales) that resembles the weird imagery and narrative fragments we find in dreams. If this insight is correct, then at least some mythic stories are 'exteriorisations' of deep subconscious processing of human experience; an attempt to 'work out' rationally the complex and sometimes confusing events of our lives. The psychologist Jerome S. Bruner touches on this point in his essay in 'Myths and Mythmaking' (Murray, 1968) when he makes the distinction between 'logos' (reasoning, rationality) and 'mythos' (tale, story) – what he calls the grammar of experience and the grammar of myth. As such, mythic stories are there to be 'absorbed'; to be processed tacitly at a subconscious level rather than being analysed rationally. It's interesting that in his book 'The Uses of Enchantment: the meaning and importance of fairy tales', the Austrian psychologist Bruno Bettelheim (Bettelheim, 1991) advises that fairy tales should simply be told to children and not explained to them, in the belief that children make what meanings they will of such stories on an individual basis: that dismantling a fairy tale is like trying to appreciate a poem by studying its individual words rather than absorbing it as an 'organic whole'. This reminds us of the fact that while people might share the symbolism of some dream images in common, many can only be interpreted individually. Joseph Campbell touches on the same topic in his 'The Way of Myth' when he says that western cultures have misunderstood myths in two important ways – by thinking that they refer to actual historical or geographical events and thinking that myths refer to supernatural fact; an attempt to impose logos on mythos. This, says Campbell, has contributed to what he calls a loss of 'the vocabulary of the spirit'.

As an aside, though a relevant one, the American researcher in psychology, Julian Jaynes, put forward a fascinating theory in his impressively titled book 'The Origin of Consciousness in the Breakdown of the Bicameral Mind' (Jaynes, 1993). Jaynes speculates that in pre-Homeric and Homeric times, the human mind was 'bicameral'; that the conscious and subconscious aspects of thinking were equally balanced and accessible. His thesis is that when characters in stories such as the Iliad and the Odyssey spoke to the gods and the gods appeared and replied, what the characters were doing was eliciting a subconscious response based on their own 'inner wisdom'. In other words, we know far more than we consciously think we know. This chimes with a theory of creativity put forward by the French mathematician Henri Poincaré, who said that the steps towards having creative ideas were –

Preparation – consciously thinking about and researching a chosen topic.
Assimilation – letting all the information 'simmer' at a subconscious level.
Illumination – the Aha! or Eureka! moment when a fresh idea springs to mind, coming as it were 'out of the blue'.
Verification – testing the insight/idea in the outside world to see if it works.

In light of all of this, we feel that because of the importance of myth, children should be introduced to them, but it should be pointed out that they are more than 'just stories' and that they have relevance in the modern world (maybe children could make some connections for themselves). We also think that myth-making is an ongoing process; that the books, films and comics of today often constitute contemporary mythic narratives that children can incorporate into their value- and belief-systems, insofar as such stories can act as templates for the way children think, feel and behave through life.

We also think that while it's valid to talk about and otherwise explore myths – i.e. to study them as one would any piece of literature – there's also value in simply letting children absorb such stories and make of them what they will – there's something in what Lewis Carroll said; 'No, no! The adventures first, explanations take such a dreadful time'.

Finally on this topic, we want to mention Alexander Eliot again who, in 'The Timeless Myths' asserts that mythic narrative underlies everything, laying the foundation for science, religion and philosophy, since its goal is to arrive at the broadest possible basis of knowledge, driven by an abiding hunger for significance within ourselves; individually, within our culture and as a species. As such, Eliot feels that what he calls the 'prove it' attitude that underpins science and rationality 'impoverishes imagination and stultifies discussion' when applied to myth (Eliot, 1997, page 61) – though in our opinion that view, if you accept it, in no way nullifies the value of science and rationality: rationality and imagination, logos and mythos, are both valuable ways of engaging with the world.

Tony – Scientific exposition can certainly slow up a narrative, as anyone who has sat through the interminable dialogue scenes in 1950s Science Fiction (SF) films will confirm; where white men in suits or white lab coats torture us with dubious scientific mumbo jumbo. What we really want to do is see the monster! (The Science Fiction writer Arthur C. Clarke advised would-be SF authors to avoid what he called 'now tell me professor' slabs of explanation.)

Activity: Ask children to think about any values or beliefs that they have come to accept and act on through reading stories (both ancient and modern). What was it about such stories that led them to take such values and beliefs 'on board'?

Legends, Fairy Tales and Folk Tales

In his book 'The Myths of Reality', author Simon Danser (2005) talks of the 'degeneration' of myths into legends and folklore, while Alexander Eliot, whom we've mentioned several times, calls legends and folktales 'light hearted derivatives' of myth. However, Eliot also feels that legends, folk tales and fairy tales, along with myths, belong to what he calls the 'mythosphere'; the whole collection of narratives and the wisdom they contain that exist across the mythical landscape. Looking back at the Ladder to the Moon (page 52), you may feel, as we do, that folk tales and legends aren't watered-down versions of mythic motifs, but steps *up* towards the deeper understanding of life's great mysteries that myths attempt to address. In line with the ladder metaphor, fairy tales and so on are as necessary to the integrity of the whole structure as origin and creation stories.

Danser makes the point that all societies have their own ideologies; their own systems of ideas and ideals, which he describes as a group of metaphors based around a root or core metaphor. He goes on to say that myths are ideologies plus narrative – stories conveying moral codes, etc. – and that 'mythic fragments' suggest and build towards these more elaborate stories. Legends, folk tales, fairy tales and even jokes and anecdotes can contain such mythic fragments.

Tony – In contemporary culture, the Marvel Cinematic Universe and similar shared universes such as the DC universe are sometimes mistakenly referred to as a modern mythology in that they too combine a variety of narratives into a complex tapestry in which fans identify and relate to common thematic elements. Fanatical though a minority of fans may be however, it hardly constitutes a belief system. It does undoubtedly incorporate mythic elements and tropes drawing on elements of existing myths and legends, most obviously with the incorporation by Marvel of Norse mythology in Thor, and Atlantis and the Amazons in films by their 'rival' comic company DC.

Steve – I remember a formidable deputy headmistress at a school where I worked telling me that a few nights earlier she was walking her dog along the main street in her village when a man in an overcoat came striding towards her. It looked as though he didn't intend to step aside to let her pass, so she stepped aside. The man went by without offering a thank you. Feeling annoyed by this discourtesy, she turned around to say something to him, except that he was nowhere in sight. He'd vanished. The deputy head's interpretation was that the man was a ghost rather than a hallucination.

This anecdote† counts as a mythic fragment because it points towards the greater realm of the paranormal, which raises deep questions about the nature of reality that challenge the current scientific paradigm (page 87) of materialism. It also raises the larger issues of the relationship between seeing and believing, and the nature of personal beliefs that influence our interpretation of what we experience. (An interesting book that explores a range of strange phenomena is 'Truly Weird' by Jenny Randles [1998]. The book is useful because it includes arguments/explanations by both sceptics and by 'believers' that the phenomena, while paranormal, are nevertheless real. Randles also gives her own views at the end of the volume.)

In his book 'The Wisdom of Fairy Tales', author Rudolph Meyer (Meyer, 1988) suggests that fairy tales have their greatest impact when read within the ethos that accommodates a love of the impossible, of the absurd and of paradox. Many children surely possess these qualities and it would be disparaging to diminish them with the label 'childlike naiveté'. As adults, with our 'rational' understanding of the world (logos), we might have to actively suspend our disbelief when confronted with the supposedly impossible, the absurd and with paradox, or indeed just react with scepticism and doubt. (In this regard, would you believe the deputy headmistress who claimed to have seen a ghost? If not, what would your interpretation be?)

Tony – Part of the great appeal of traditional tales is their lack of logic, where wonderful things just happen and where anything is possible! Why can't there be a magic tinderbox hidden in an old tree that can summon three magical hounds?

A Controversy

Author Peter Laws in 'The Frighteners: why we love monsters, ghosts, death and gore' (Laws, 2018) explores the controversy surrounding the view of some parents that children shouldn't be exposed to fairy tales for a variety of reasons. One of these touches on the use of the word 'dwarf' in 'Snow White', which some people find offensive. Checking online, however, we find that while the word 'midget' is widely considered to be

---

† Anecdote comes from the Greek *anekdota*, which means 'unpublished'. The original sense of the word in English was 'secret or private stories'.

a slur, dwarf and dwarfism seem to be less emotionally charged and are more acceptable – though the littlepeopleofontario.com website (accessed February 2022) points out very reasonably that 'people of short stature' prefer to be called by their names rather than by a generalised label.

Another point of contention is that some adults feel many fairy tales are 'too scary' for children: laws cites one survey which found that 20% of respondents refused to read 'Hansel and Gretel' to their children because, at one point, the children are abandoned in the forest. A more recent survey carried out by the makers of the US fantasy-crime series 'Grimm' found that a third of respondents refused to read 'The Gingerbread Man' because he gets eaten by a fox at the end. Nearly half of parents avoided 'Rumpelstiltskin' because the story involves kidnapping and execution.

These and other surveys sparked fierce debate in the media. Laws quotes child development expert Sally Goddard Blythe who appeared in the Telegraph newspaper, where she argued that traditional fairy tales were 'crucial to children's development' because they taught moral behaviour and were honest about humanity, showcasing as they do the strengths and weaknesses of human beings. Also, the use of good and evil stereotypes throws up a clear moral code that children can follow in their own lives. Writer Ellie Levenson agrees, arguing that if parents don't want their children to talk to strangers and avoid other possible dangers, then children need frames of reference for what might happen if they aren't cautious. Peter Laws makes the very valid point that as children grow up, they'll be exposed to many disturbing news stories and inevitably meet unpleasant people anyway and that if they're not prepared for these things, then 'they'll be in for a shock'.

In an educational context, the issue is more complicated. While parents have the right not to expose their children to what they regard as inappropriate fairy tales, as teachers we can't just simply go ahead and tell them, if we accept Laws' reasoning and that of the people he quotes. Perhaps some discussion and policy decisions would be the safest way to proceed. We find it ironic, however, that the brothers Grimm sanitised/bowdlerised many of the tales they collected, watering down what the darkforestfairytales.blogspot.com refers to as the 'dark material' of the original stories. If you want to explore the matter further, a useful short article can be found at https://www.bbc.com/culture/article/20130801-too-grimm-for-children.

A Hierarchy of Understandings

Many of the points we've made in this section touch upon a theory put forward by the educational philosopher Kieran Egan in his book 'The Educated Mind: how cognitive tools shape our understanding' (Egan,

1998). He suggests that as we grow, we pass through different stages in the way we perceive and understand the world. These are –

Somatic understanding. The innate 'understanding' of one's physical functions and of one's emotions; so hot-cold, hungry-thirsty, happy-sad, for example. Such understanding comes before language acquisition.
Mythic understanding. This occurs during the development of 'grammatical language' (two to six years) and takes the form of appreciating binary opposites such as tall-short, good-evil, etc. Images, metaphors and narrative structure are ways in which this kind of understanding operates and develops.
Romantic understanding. The word 'romantic' is not used in the sense of romantic love, but describes the stage of understanding where children search for the limits of reality and take an interest in the transcendent qualities of things – those attributes that go beyond the range of normal human experience.
Philosophic understanding. This is the level of understanding reached in adulthood, where the world is perceived through a web of concepts; where accepted patterns and principles are used to organise knowledge, perceptions and experiences; the 'logos' mentioned earlier.

If our networks of concepts and beliefs go unquestioned however, then we can become resistant to new ideas that challenge what we believe the world to be like. Authors Neil Postman and Charles Weingartner in their fine book 'Teaching as a Subversive Activity' (Postman and Weingartner, 1972) call this a 'hardening of the categories'. We'll be looking at this topic later in the section on scientific narratives.

Luckily, understanding doesn't necessarily stop evolving there ...

Ironic understanding. This is expressed as a preparedness to look critically at one's beliefs; to treat facts – and more broadly the narratives we encounter – as human constructs; to bring an open-minded scepticism to what we experience and the language we use to describe it: in other words, to have the flexibility to consider alternative philosophic explanations. These can effectively be examined through Socratic dialogue in the form of philosophical enquiries, which we looked at on page 51. Children's acceptance that fictional narratives can 'tell us something true' and that facts are provisional, given that further information might modify or invalidate them, together with a playful attitude towards ideas and a questioning attitude, is an important step in developing an ironic understanding of the world.

Wonderment and the Wisdom of Fairy Tales

Children are not only naturally curious but open to the wonder the world can bring; seeing things with a sense of what the educationalist Margaret Meek calls 'firstness'.

Steve – for instance, when I visit schools I tell children how, when I was a child, I would play with my friends out on the hills above my coal-mining village in South Wales. We'd also trek up to the slag heap at the top of the hill and search for fossils and chunks of quartz. I show examples of these that I collected back then; the fossilised leaves of a fern, impressions of tree bark, a lump of quartz. I point out that these fossilised plants were alive long before the dinosaurs appeared. It gratifies me that young children literally gasp with wonder, whereas older pupils usually don't. Author Rudolf Meyer in his 'The Wisdom of Fairy Tales' almost pleads for us as adults to cultivate and preserve the sense of wonder that children are born with, suggesting that exposing them to fairy tales facilitates this and 'gives life to the power of imagination'.

Activity: According to vocabulary.com (accessed December 2021), the word 'wonder' comes from the Old English *wundor* and means 'a marvellous thing, the object of astonishment' (Oxford Languages adds that the ultimate origin of the word is unknown). Discuss with the class what it means for something to be 'wonderful'. What do the children themselves find to be wonderful? What does it mean to be astonished? What qualities does something need to possess for it to be called marvellous? (You may wish to link this with the notion of romantic understanding on page 61.) Have any of the children read stories that have filled them with wonder? If so, what was it about those stories that evoked that emotion? Have they had any experiences that have evoked wonder?

Activity: 'Wonder' can also be used in the sense of wondering about something; pondering, puzzling. Perhaps most of us wonder at times about life's 'big questions', which we looked at on page 52. Discussing these (even without the formal structure of a philosophical enquiry) can be tantalising and even exhilarating. Opening a lesson with a deep question not only stimulates the imagination but hones children's critical thinking and questioning skills. 'Curriculum pressure' permitting, you might entice children with questions such as –

How can we know if something is real?
Are thoughts real?
What does it mean to think?
How do we know that something is alive?

What makes us human?
What is a feeling and why do we have them?
Could an artificially intelligent machine ever have feelings?
Is a person made up of only a body and a mind?
Does the brain create the mind, or allow it to express itself (in the same way that a TV set 'expresses' programmes)?
Is seeing believing?
What is goodness and how do we know that something is good? (Include different nuances of goodness; a good meal, a good book, a good laugh, etc.)
What does it mean to be wise?
Is it always wrong to lie?
Is it always wrong to steal?

If you decide to build 'deep question time' into the school day, invite children to offer other topics that *they* wonder about. See also 'frontiers of science' on pages 88 and 98.

Note: Nowadays the use of superlatives is commonplace. Ordinary things are 'absolutely fabulous', celebrities are 'icons', 'legends' and 'national treasures', an idea can be 'genius' or 'awesome' or 'epic' and so on. Hyperbole (from the Greek meaning 'excess') and exaggeration when overused can diminish the power of the language. Discussing ideas such as wonderment and wonderful alerts children to the truer meaning and significance of these terms and perhaps dampens the tendency to use them casually.

Activity: Work with the class to make a list of fairy tales that children have listened to or read for themselves. Split the class into pairs or small groups. Ask each group to pick a fairy tale and identify the motifs that feature in it (also see page 15). If 36 motifs are collected, they can be put into a 6 × 6 grid. Children can then either cherry pick to create their own fairy tale or 'take their minds by surprise' using dice rolls (page 23). Alternatively, they can select from the motifs offered here and/or use dice rolls.

Working with Grids

Here are four 6 × 6 grids featuring further fairy tale motifs. Use these as in the activity above (if children struggle to make a grid of their own). You might also consider running the subsidiary activities in the following section. These will familiarise children with a greater number of motifs and also allow them to practise different thinking skills (Figure 2.2).

Opposites. Ask children to pick pairs of words that are opposites – descend/ascend, uncharted/way, learner/mentor, for instance.

Adventurer	Guide	Wise one	Prince(ss)	Ruler	Witch
Guardian	Wanderer	Hero(ine)	Beast	Enchanter	Lover
Keeper	Captor	Liberator	Learner	Mentor	Companion
Trial	Quest	Mirror	Blade	Barrier	Road
Gift	Theft	Descend	Ascend	Earth	Air
Fire	Water	Metal	Wood	Stone	Coincidence

Circle	Pattern	Order	Chaos	Disguise	Mountain
Lake	Shore	Threshold	Woods	Darkness	Light
Tower	Labyrinth	Bridge	Dwelling	City	Door
Key	Hut / hovel	Palace	Uncharted	High seas	Life/death
Sleep	Wish	Bond	Mother	Father	Siblings
Trickster	Maker	Giant	Creature	Bird	Fish

Serpent	Tree	Seed	Crown	Mantle	Sphere
Talisman	Touchstone	Bowl	Weapon	Wand	Crystal
Word	Dance	Number	Moon	Stars	Sun
Time	Edge	Axis	Centre	Transform	Betrayal
Abandon	Save	Body	Blood	Flesh	Egg
Essence	Pact	Promise	Faith	Doubt	Mind

Dream	Feeling	Game	Goal	Journey	Destiny
Puzzle	Growth	Healing	Help	Opposite	Act
Stillness	Identity	Imagine	Inner	Outer	Ladder
Hierarchy	Memory	Origin	Ritual	Split	Wholeness
Theft	Union	Unknown	Wheel	Web	Age
Way	Higher	Lower	Space	Omen	Lock

Figure 2.2 Motifs Grids.

Linked words. Ask children to find pairs or clusters of words that are connected in some way – beast, bird, fish, serpent, for example.

Word distinctions. Pick two or more similar words and ask the children to discuss/research how they differ – captor/keeper, threshold/door, road/way, for instance.

Combinations. Ask children to pick two or three words from the grid to create possible story titles (also see page 38) – Keeper of the Blade, Quest for the Crystal, Bloodstone, The Time Mirror, etc. What storylines do these titles suggest?

Categories. Have children pick out words that relate to groups of things, then other items from the grids (plus further examples they think of) that fit within those categories. Creature – bird, fish, serpent, for instance. Take it further by asking children to find words that fit into categories they make up – earth, air, fire, water (elements)/ascend, descend, higher, lower (directions).

Associations. Working individually, in pairs or in groups, children pick a word and then spend a few minutes doing 'free association/brainstorming to create an association chain or web. They can move away from fairy tales here if they wish – shore, line, sand, seaside, paddling, kites, candyfloss, ice cream, seagulls …

Parts of speech. Pick a word and think about how it can be used as different parts of speech in various sentences, so for instance 'Mark' – The prince made a mark on the paper. The hero was marked by the creature's claws. The quest led the wanderer to the mark stone.

Etymology. Ask children to research the origin of words they select from the grid and to note related words. Destiny for example comes from the Latin meaning 'to make firm' or 'establish', the idea being that which has been established or set by fate. 'Destination' is a linked word.

Activity: Here are some more common motifs that feature in fairy tales, together with suggestions for what they could symbolise (see also pages 22 and 135). Hold back from revealing the motifs' symbolic meaning and ask the children to offer their own ideas.

Dragons – represent strength and ferocity and, in Eastern cultures, wisdom.

Fairies – represent innocence and a happy-go-lucky attitude. In older traditions, however, such as Celtic, fairies are darker and can be deceitful and malevolent.

Knights – represent courage and other noble qualities, and protectiveness.

Royalty – represents power, wealth and prestige.

Unicorns – usually represent purity and gentleness.

Wolves – can represent savagery and threat (for example, in 'Little Red Riding Hood'). They also embody the spirit of the wild.

Activity: Ask the children to come up with modern equivalents of people, creatures or objects that embody the symbolism contained in some traditional motifs. Can children now use these to create a 'contemporary fairy tale'? So dragons could become weapons or AI computers; fairies, the friendly sort, could be represented by social media likes; while the trickster-fairies could transform into scammers or other kinds of deceitful people. Alternatively, children could use these motifs in a traditional way but within a modern setting – a fairy tale for the 21st century, if not a myth!

Activity: Ask children to think about and discuss whether or how fairy tales are relevant to the modern day, giving examples if they can.

Include parables and 'teaching tales'. 'Parable' by the way comes from the Greek meaning 'throwing alongside' in the sense of a comparison, allegory or illustration. Parables have been called metaphors in story form, while proverbs (page 79) have been termed parables in miniature; one-sentence stories – 'The wit of one and the wisdom of many' (attrib. Lord John Russell).

An obvious example is 'Little Red Riding Hood', which advises us not to wander off 'the straight and narrow path', and to beware of dangers that are hidden or disguised.

Another example is a story from the Zen tradition telling of a wealthy man who had everything he wanted and believed he had experienced the best the world had to offer. One day he was riding across a meadow when a tiger appeared and began to chase him. His frightened horse bolted uncontrollably and headed towards a cliff edge. Realising his danger a moment too late, the man jumped off the horse (which swerved away), rolled over the edge but managed to grab a tough old strawberry plant growing out of a crevice. A moment later the tiger's head loomed over the brink. To the man's horror, the roots of the plant began to tear away from the cliff. Despite his fear of imminent death, the man noticed a single ripe strawberry growing within reach. In his final moments before he fell, he plucked the fruit and popped it into his mouth. It was the finest thing he had ever tasted.

If you tell this story to the children, ask them what the moral of it is, perhaps framing it as 'what lessons did the man learn from this experience?' To our mind the story teaches that life is sometimes unpredictable and dangerous; that it's easy to take things for granted, or not to fully appreciate the simple gifts and pleasures of life. Could we also stretch the point to include 'you don't know what you've got until you're about to lose it'?

Incidentally, in his book 'Zen Flesh, Zen Bones', author Paul Reps (Reps, 1980) has compiled dozens of similar short tales. Many of these can be understood immediately, but others take the form of koans. These are paradoxes that confound the logical mind and are used by students of Zen in their meditation. Perhaps the most famous example is, 'what is the sound of one hand clapping?' The tendency is to try to 'work it out' rationally, except that it can't be done or else throws up facile responses such as 'well, one hand clapping doesn't make a sound'. It would be interesting to put this puzzler to the children: although we've never done it, we suspect that younger children might offer more intuitive and even nonsensical responses – and rightly so. Some children might just giggle, and this too is a very acceptable reply. The great populariser of Zen and Taoist philosophies, Alan Watts, reached the stage in his later years when, if he was asked about the meaning of life, or to respond to one of the other big existential questions, he would simply chuckle like a little kid. This indicates the depth of his understanding – and we are in no way being ironic, in the ordinary sense of the term only.

By the way, although the tradition of Zen is linked to Buddhism, it can also be regarded, as we've suggested, as a philosophical system designed to lead a more fulfilling and happier life, offering a philosophical understanding of the world (page 61), but leading beyond that to an ironic (looking back and questioning) attitude.

Parables also exist at the interface between philosophy and science. One of the most famous (some sources call it an allegory) is that of Plato's Cave. In one version, the Greek philosopher Plato posits a cave in which prisoners are chained together. Behind the prisoners is a fire, and between the prisoners and the fire are people carrying puppets and other objects, casting shadows on the wall of the cave, which the prisoners believe to be real. If a prisoner somehow became free, he would see the fire and know that the shadows aren't real. If then he escaped from the cave, he would find the real world, realising that another and deeper level of reality existed. The scientific/philosophical underpinning of this story raises the issue of what reality actually is, and our interpretations and beliefs about it.

Plato's Cave is a kind of thought experiment; one that can be carried out in the imagination but, for whatever reason, not in reality. The theoretical physicist Albert Einstein, in formulating his theory of relativity, imagined moving alongside a beam of light (the Wikipedia article on Einstein's thought experiments lists several more). This flight of the imagination brought breakthrough insights that took his thinking forward.

Bruno Bettelheim, who we mentioned earlier, felt that fairy tales, folktales and parables raise problems and offer solutions (and in the case of koans, prompt a shift in perception and attitude). Thus, Bettelheim suggests that such stories provide 'inner resources' to help people deal with what he calls universal human problems – including the ever-present moral problem of dealing with evil – but also individual issues and crises such as, in his view; overcoming selfishness and narcissism, dealing with family issues and sibling rivalries, becoming able to 'relinquish childhood dependencies' and evolving a sense of moral obligation.

Alexander Eliot in 'The Timeless Myths' mirrors Bettelheim's insistence on the value of myths and fairy tales, acknowledging that human beings make mistakes and yet despite this he suggests that such stories carry powerful messages – that light shines in the darkness, frontiers open to fresh vistas, love follows hard upon conflict and discord and that from what is hidden comes revelation.

In his book 'The Myth Gap: what happens when evidence and arguments aren't enough?' (Evans, 2017), the author highlights and bemoans the current rational-materialistic attitude of 'literal or not' (very like the 'prove it' attitude mentioned on page 57), rather than taking a dual perspective in learning life's lessons (accommodating both logos and mythos), thus leading to the 'myth gap' of the book's title, which echoes Joseph Campbell's view that western societies have become 'demythologised'.

Steve – Such a dual perspective is exemplified in a story my wife once told me. She was on playground duty at the children's nursery where she worked, when she noticed one of the children, Samantha, pushing a pram along and talking to the doll it contained. Wishing to join in with the little girl's play, my wife went over and also spoke to the doll, at which point Samantha tutted, looked critically at her and said condescendingly, 'Wendy, it's just a lump of plastic!' Such is the comingling and easy accommodation of so many children's inner and outer worlds.

Folklore

Even if we accept Simon Danser's assertion that myths 'degenerate' into legends and folklore (page 58), this does not diminish the value of such narratives in offering useful – not just entertaining – messages about life. As an instance of this, Robert and Michéle Root-Bernstein's book 'Honey Mud Maggots and Other Medical Marvels' (Root-Bernstein, 1999) details the scores of instances where traditional folk remedies and treatments have been found to be effective, with many modern medicines and procedures evolving out of this ancient wisdom. The word 'lore' incidentally comes from the Old English term for 'instruction' and is linked to the German for 'learn', which cycles us back to the notion that even fictional narratives can tell us something true, or at least something of practical value.

Activity: A quick online search (or glancing through Root-Bernsteins' book) will reveal many cases of folkloric wisdom proving to be effective in modern medicine. Giving groups of children the task of researching a few of these will emphasise the point that folklore sometimes amounts to more than just superstition, and will also offer insight into the history of medicine.

A fascinating sidelight on these ideas relates to Noam Chomsky's theory of Universal Grammar. Chomsky, an American linguist, philosopher and cognitive scientist, proposed that the ability to learn and understand language is 'hard wired' into the human brain; i.e. that it has a genetic component and so is innate. The theory is controversial and not universally accepted by linguists (in fact. E. O. Wilson in 'The Origins of Creativity' states that Chomsky's theory has, through lack of evidence, been largely abandoned by researchers of linguistic psychology, though James Le Fanu in 'Why Us?' [Le Fanu, 2010, Chapter 2] argues robustly in its favour). Chomsky's theory does chime with the notion that human intelligence is also innate – that people are born with 'intelligence potential'; with the capacity to acquire and apply knowledge and skills, and by extension with the notion that we are also born with the potential to develop our ability to experience, perceive and understand the world as a series of interconnected stories and to make sense generally of life by developing a coherent world view (what we might call a 'metanarrative'). The word intelligence comes from a Latin term meaning to understand. These ideas relate to speculations posed by the American folklorist Alan Dundes in his introduction to the second edition of Propp's 'The Morphology of the Folktale'. In this, Dundes wonders how children come to understand the structure of folktales and fairy tales in the first place. It's unlikely that children consciously think about the deep narrative structure of such stories but rather that they absorb common themes, elements and motifs tacitly, that are then assimilated subconsciously. If this is the case, then it supports the notion of simply *telling* children folk and fairy tales instead of explaining and analysing them, at least sometimes.

Dundes goes on to ponder this very idea, wondering if children unconsciously extrapolate fairy tale morphology through hearing many individual fairy tales. This seems reasonable enough in our opinion, though we think that the ability of children to understand stories of many kinds operates through the broader processes of an evolving ability to 'read' the world through narratives.

Activity: Dundes suggests an interesting experiment to test children's understanding of fairy tales and folk tales; by reading part of a non-traditional (i.e. unfamiliar) fairy tale to the children and then ask them to finish the story. Children's ability to do this in a logically consistent way – so that the whole story is rounded off and makes sense – indicates that at some level they understand basic narrative elements (page 8), the narrative template (page 18) and the part played by narrative motifs (page 64). Trying this out with the class would be a useful test of children's creativity, while comparing their story endings with the actual tale would be fascinating.

Activity: Another activity for exploring children's knowledge and understanding of such stories is by playing what we call the 'stackers' game, as shown in Figure 2.3. Begin with a simple sentence that features two or three fairy tale motifs, such as 'A giant captured the king's daughter'.

One version of the game asks children to put an adjective before each noun. So for example 'An evil giant captured the old king's beautiful daughter'. Now link an adverb to the verb – 'An evil giant stealthily captured the old king's beautiful daughter'. Other phrases and clauses can be added to turn a simple sentence into a complex one.

	trickster	deceived		Emperor's	treasurer
	wizard	entranced		Queen's	servant
	dragon	advised		Prince's	brother
A	giant	captured	the	King's	daughter

Figure 2.3 Stackers.

The 'stacking' idea is to take each of the motifs of the original sentence and to think of alternatives, placing them in columns above the original …

Help children to do this task successfully by showing them the motifs grids on page 64.

Playing with motifs in this way develops children's creative thinking skills and increases their familiarity with folk and fairy tales, while using a sentence such as 'A quick brown fox jumps over the lazy dog' helps to familiarise children with the parts of speech. (That example by the way is a pangram, a sentence that contains all of the letters of the alphabet. Because it is one of the shortest to do so, and is coherent, it is one of the most widely known.)

Local Folktales

We suspect that every region, county and even neighbourhood has its own treasure chest of folktales. While some of these might fit with the kinds of stories that 'tell you something true', others will be based on beliefs of the time and corruptions or misinterpretations of historical events and natural phenomena.

In our neck of the woods (which we went down to today and received a big surprise), a very famous folk tale features the evil witch Black Annis, who lived in a small cave excavated in the soft stone of the Dane Hills, which lie to the west of Leicester. Annis's favourite food was any child foolish enough to wander too close to her cavern after dark. In a sense this story conveys the 'real life messages' of being extra vigilant if out at night, and keeping clear of forbidden or supposedly dangerous locales (Do not step over the line! Page 8).

An online search will likely bring up many folk tales for your area, while booklets of such stories can often be found in local Tourist Information centres and bookshops. Encouraging children to research local folk lore helps them to understand the narrative structure of such tales and teaches them something about the area in which they live (though be aware of the controversy surrounding the topic of fairy tales, folk tales, etc. See page 58).

Urban Folk Tales

Urban folktales, also called urban myths, legends or 'friend of a friend' (FOAF) stories, belong to a class of narratives that often cause shock and/or amusement and that usually sound believable. Many are set in the recent past and happen to 'ordinary' people that we can identify with. In his book 'Curses! Broiled Again!', American folklorist Jan Harold Brunvand (Brunvand, 1990) suggests that FOAF tales are believed partly because listeners hear them from several sources – 'These people can't all be wrong, so there must be some truth in it'. You might, by the way, want to put that idea to the children to find out if they doubt the reasoning: one tactic in philosophy is to use sheer numbers of people to bolster a point of view – the ad populum move.

Urban folktales demonstrate that folklore is as alive and kicking today as it has ever been, and that the dissemination of such stories, via the internet and social media, is wider and more rapid than ever before. The usefulness of urban folk stories, apart from their entertainment value, is that many of them serve as cautionary tales that help to mould people's behaviour, or at least give people pause for thought before making a possibly unfortunate decision. In common with narratives found in the Horror genre, urban myths also allow the acknowledgement and expression of people's fear by 'naming the darkness'. Further, such stories bring an educational benefit insofar as they allow us to think critically and, as it were, recalibrate our gullibility settings. This is important, since being gullible can make us vulnerable, especially if narratives are convincingly told, especially by someone with charisma and authority, or from a supposedly trustworthy source. On the other hand, urban legends often give good advice set in a fictional and entertaining framework. Interestingly, classic writers of ghostly tales such as Sheridan le Fanu and, later, M. R. James often employed the technique of a story being recounted second or third hand, just as many urban legends happened to someone else the person telling the tale will know.

Tantalisingly, the origins of most urban folktales are elusive and mysterious. In another of his books, 'The Vanishing Hitchhiker: urban legends and their meanings' (Brunvand, 1983), as well as in 'Curses! Broiled Again!', Brunvand tells us that he has on many occasions tried to track down the source of some of the stories, with few exceptions without success. Most usually contemporary stories are retellings of older tales that themselves blur and vanish into the 'mists of time' (forgive the cliché). At this point, we'll also mention that Brunvand makes a distinction between what he calls 'narrative folklore' – folkloric information that acquires a clear storyline – and urban legends, which are stories alleged to be true.

One of the most enduring and well-known urban legends is that of the phantom or vanishing hitchhiker. There are many variations of this tale going back generations, but the bare bones of the story are that a man is driving home late one night when he sees a thin, pale young woman standing at the side of the road. He offers her a lift, which she accepts. She gets into the back of the car and asks if he can take her home, giving the driver her address. Because the girl looks so wan, the man glances in his rearview mirror occasionally to check that she's OK. At one point he looks and can't see her, supposing that she's lain down to sleep, or has fainted. Being concerned she might be ill, he pulls over to check on her only to discover that she's vanished. Now he worries and retraces his route to see if, somehow, the girl has fallen out of the car. He fails to find her. He then drives to the address the girl gave him. An older woman answers the door. After the driver has told his story, the woman informs him that she is the girl's mother, but that her daughter died in a road accident some years ago, at the very spot where the driver picked her up.

Reading this through, it's easy to dismiss the tale as 'just another ghost story'. But think back to the anecdote that the formidable headmistress told Steve (page 58) about the phantom dog walker. If someone you knew and, especially, respected, told you the story of the vanishing hitchhiker with utter conviction that it was true, would you not be tempted to believe it, especially if the teller claimed it had happened to them, or a close friend of theirs?

One indicator that the story isn't true, or didn't happen to the teller or a friend of a friend, is that essentially similar hitchhiker stories are to be found all over the world going back decades, according to Michael Goss in his book 'The Evidence for Phantom Hitchhikers' (Goss, 1984).

The variants of story of the phantom girl (which Brunvand points out is one of many 'automobile legends') contain a number of stable elements, namely; driver, time and place, hitchhiker, her address, her choice of seat, her disappearance, driver's concern, identification of the girl by a parent and news of her death.

Activity: Many urban folktales aren't suitable for children; we'll mention a few that are later. But the phantom hitchhiker we think is gentle enough for children to hear. If you tell it to the class, mention the stable elements above and ask children to construct their version of the story, featuring themselves if they wish, together with any other features to make it more believable.

Activity: Ask children to imagine that they could interview the driver of the car. What questions would they ask him about the incident to try and ascertain its veracity? (Note that according to Goss, in stories where the driver is male, the hitchhiker is female and vice versa.)

Tony – Often whoever is recounting the urban legend links it to a real place giving it a bogus verisimilitude. I can recall being told of a particularly frightening incident involving a friend of a friend, taking place in a car park in Kettering. Later I was told of an identical encounter, involving a different person, in a shopping mall car park in Canada! Car parks, it seems, are dangerous places! Another cautionary tale then?

Activity: The 'belief-ometer'. Ask children to decide, using a scale of 1–10, how far they believe the story of the phantom hitchhiker, giving reasons for their decision. You can take the activity further by asking them to assess other ghost stories and/or urban folktales. Goss suggests that narrative touches such as exaggeration and shocking details (what he calls 'artificial colouring') might lead a critical thinker to doubt the veracity of the story, though these touches don't per se disprove the existence of ghosts generally. Goss talks about 'criteria of reliability' which can be used as tools for assessing urban folktales (and, we would argue, narratives in other domains). In the case of the phantom hitchhiker, he mentions embellishments and shocking details, inconsistencies, preconceived ideas about ghosts, lack of corroboration, the possibility of misinterpretation or self-delusion.

We think that this is an important activity when it comes to applying critical thinking to mis- and disinformation, fake news and conspiracy theories.

Steve – As an adjunct to the above, and in preparation for the following activities, I'd like to mention that I've had a few what might be called paranormal experiences; or at least incidents that I can't explain (explain away?) rationally. The most startling concerned a llama, Mr Finn, that my wife and I once owned. He lived in a small paddock at the back of our house and slept in an old wooden outhouse. One day he became very agitated and died painfully (with no help from the ineffectual vet who arrived long after we'd made an emergency phone call to him). We were of course deeply distressed that our pet had suffered so much. Months later I was washing dishes (yes, really) in the kitchen that overlooked the paddock when I happened to glance up. There in the shadowy doorway of the outhouse, where Mr Finn had lived, was what I can only describe as a 'floating luminescence'; a patch of light that was the same tan colour, shape and height as our llama's head when standing. There were no other details to it. I simply stood and watched it for long moments until it withdrew into the darkness of the outhouse and vanished. I use the word 'withdrew' deliberately – the patch of light moved slowly backwards into the building and faded. I count myself to be a fairly level-headed and rational man and thought through various possibilities. The event occurred during a sunny autumn afternoon with excellent visibility. The sun was low in the southwest, to my left, but not obscured in any way by trees. There was a light wind and little cloud. There was no way that what I saw was a trick of the light. Also I had not been thinking about the llama nor, as far as I recall, was agitated about anything. Nor had I yet partaken of my daily medicinal small glass of red wine ... The experience, nor anything like it, has ever recurred.

The interpretation that I put on the experience at that time was that Mr Finn, or some manifestation of him, had shown itself to me as if to say, 'It's OK, don't feel bad because I'm all right now'. I didn't tell my wife about it for weeks, or any of our friends for many months. I'm open minded and undecided about the existence of ghosts and some other aspects of the paranormal, but when something like this happens to one personally, it does prompt a reexamination of beliefs.

(At this point you might reflect on why this is not an urban folk tale.) There are a few other points to note about Steve's experience –

The event itself and Steve's interpretation of it are not the same thing, but –

His interpretation of what he saw made sense to him of all aspects of the experience.

He feels that the matter-of-fact nature of the experience adds to its veracity.

Activity: Ask the children whether or how strongly they believe (a) Steve's account and (b) his interpretation of what caused it. Would children be more inclined to believe it if one of their family or a close friend had had the experience? Also ask what assumptions, presuppositions or judgements went into their view, explaining these terms as necessary.

As we'll explore in the section on scientific narratives, we tend to perceive and interpret events based on our personal belief systems. As various commentators have noted, we don't see the world as it is but as *we* are. As such, because Steve likes to think of himself as open minded, although emotionally he holds on to his interpretation of 'the llama incident', he's perfectly prepared to consider other possible explanations.

Activity: If you want to share this anecdote with the class, ask the children to come up with possible explanations. How is Steve's experience similar to/different from that of the deputy headmistress and the phantom dog walker?

As an adjunct to the activity, you can offer children the etymologies of related words, or get the children to research them for themselves.

Apparition – Middle English, 'the action of appearing', from Latin 'attendance'.

Ghost – Old English *gast* meaning 'spirit or soul', also 'breath'.

Phantom – Middle English, 'illusion, delusion', from Greek 'to make visible, to show'.

Incidentally, while thinking on this topic, we checked up on illusions, delusions and hallucinations. An illusion is usually an innocent trick of the imagination‡; a delusion is a false belief; and a hallucination is an erroneous sensory perception. All are examples of false reality – Now there's a topic for discussion!

Presumably such conceptions and assumptions arise, in materialistic terms, simply from electrochemical activity in the brain – as does the 'we' that creates them. Note the philosophical deep waters here. One aspect of this is the word 'trick' – meaning to deceive. We wonder what is the survival value of a brain evolving that can deceive 'us' (itself?).

Rumours Revisited and Superstitions

The word rumour comes from the Latin for 'noise' and means a currently circulating story of doubtful veracity. The entry on the Wikipedia website states that one characteristic of rumours (based on the ideas of psychologist Robert H. Knapp) is that they are spread by word of mouth. However, especially in the complex modern world of social media, mis- and disinformation, fake news, post-truth and conspiracy theories (we'll look at these later), we feel that rumours can also be spread digitally in written form and through pictures, video reports, blogs, etc. It's also the case that stories passing from person to person can become distorted in all kinds of ways …

Activity: The whispers game. Ask for a volunteer and give the child a paragraph-long message, whispering it to the child rather than writing it down. The volunteer then whispers the message to a neighbour, who passes it on to another child until it has circulated around the class. Now compare the final version with the original message and flag up any embellishments, exaggerations or other alterations. Don't explain beforehand that these can occur.

Rumours can be counted as gossip and over-the-fence tales, using our ladder to the moon analogy (page 52). They are frequently earthy tales and often concern celebrities/famous people. Knapp in his 1944 book 'A Psychology of Rumour' suggests that many rumours fall into three categories; pipe-dream rumours that reflect people's desires and wished-for outcomes; fear rumours that play on people's anxieties; and wedge-driving rumours designed to undermine group loyalty and

---

‡ Scientifically, this is explained as 'a result of our conceptions and assumptions about the world, which we impose upon visual stimuli. This can lead to four types of cognitive illusions: ambiguous illusions, distorting/geometrical-optical illusions, paradox illusions or fictions.

relationships. Some people may also take secret pleasure from hearing of the misfortunes of others; a kind of revenge by proxy.

Activity: Ask if the children know of any (non-defamatory) rumours and if so, whether they believe them and why. If reasons are forthcoming, they may highlight some of the 'moves' that feature in arguments – Appeal to authority ('if so-and-so says it, it must be true'); appeal to popularity ('so many people believe this, so it's got to be true'); appeal to celebrity ('they're famous, so they must know what they're talking about'); appeal to antiquity ('it's been around so long it must be true).

Tony – Sometimes it might be none of these. People might believe a rumour simply because for them it must be true, with no reasons to support it (the 'just because it is' position), or conversely people might be in complete denial and nothing will ever sway them from their belief (the 'hardening of the categories' position, page 61).

Strength of Reasons

One way of highlighting the value of reasons and reasoning is to offer children a morally dubious scenario and pin several reasons to it that vary in 'reasonability'. For instance, suppose a character we'll call Ben comes across a wallet lying on the pavement of a quiet street. No one is around. He looks in the wallet and finds £100 in cash. He decides to keep the money rather than take the wallet to the police. Here are some reasons he might offer for his actions. Ask children to rate them on a scale of 1–5, with one being a weak or questionable reason and five being a strong reason (this exercise is independent of the fact that it's morally wrong for Ben to keep the money).

1 I can buy myself some new video games.
2 The wallet is expensive so the person who dropped it can easily afford on £100
3 I can buy my grandmother some presents. She's been ill lately.
4 Finders keepers, losers weepers.
5 Possession is 90% of the law.
6 Dad's just lost his job and this money will be useful.
7 If I lost money, I wouldn't expect anyone to hand it in.
8 It's only money.
9 Our cat's not well and this will pay his vet's bill.
10 I'll keep half and give the other half to charity.

Invite children to think of other reasons and then rate them using the 1–5 scale. Ask children to think about what they would do in Ben's shoes (they won't need to reveal if they'd keep the money in real life!).

Ask if they can think of a compelling reason for handing the money in to the police, such as

There's an address in the wallet.
There's a photograph of an elderly person.
There's a photograph of a person with a visible disability.
There's a family photo.
There's a photograph of a cute family pet.

Ask children to think about whether the decision they make about the money would be different if the amount was £500 rather than £100.

With regard to this issue, do any of the children *feel* it's wrong for Ben to keep the money? If yes, ask them to explore this feeling. Would it be a feeling of guilt about keeping the cash, or anxiety in case someone found out, etc.? More broadly, does a feeling ever count as a valid reason for making a moral decision? Does a feeling ever count as a reason to believe or disbelieve something? Is seeing always believing? (During Steve's llama experience on page 73, he had a strong *feeling* that his interpretation was correct, i.e. that he'd experienced something paranormal; 'beyond the normal'. Note though that the term 'normal' has its roots in the current scientific paradigm of what constitutes reality and, therefore, defines what counts as normal.)

By the way, an interesting article about urban myths in education can be found at https://www.nicemedia.co.uk/myth-busting-urban-myths-about-learning-and-education-2/

Superstitions

The word derives from the Latin for 'standing over'; the Oxford Languages website suggests that this may relate to the idea of 'standing over something in awe'.

Activity: Ask children what superstitions they know about. Create a list. Some common superstitions include –

Not walking under a ladder.
Throwing salt over your shoulder if you spill some.
Touching wood to avert misfortune.
Not walking on the cracks in the pavement.
Believing that breaking a mirror will bring you seven years' bad luck.
Keeping a penny you find on the ground because it brings good luck.
Believing that misfortune is more likely to occur on Friday the 13th.

Believing that keeping a horseshoe above your front door repels misfortune.
Crossing your fingers to encourage good luck or to ensure a lie won't be found out.

Ask if the validity of any of the superstitions can be supported by reasons. For instance, not walking under a ladder lessens your chance of somebody working on it dropping something on your head. So is that being superstitious or just using caution and common sense? Can any other superstitions in the list be labelled in the same way?

Tony – I remember being told by someone that if you spill salt you had to throw a pinch over your left shoulder; but my friend had no idea why. Later he discovered that evidently it will stop the devil creeping up behind you after you'd spilt the salt – although why the devil cared so much about spilt salt, always crept up on the left (the 'sinister' side as opposed to the right, 'dexter', side) or indeed was so easily disposed of, was never clear! Steve – Maybe it's to avoid being a-salt-ed by the devil.

Activity: Ask if any of the children are superstitious, and if they have any reasons to support that belief. This might bring up the broader issue that sometimes we believe something because an adult or our friends believe it too.

Explain to the class what it means to be credulous, i.e. having the tendency to readily believe in something without evidence. Contrast this with the notions of scepticism and cynicism. Scepticism is the tendency to doubt (from the Greek for 'inquiry' or 'doubt'). Scepticism can be open-minded – I'll hold off making a decision until I have more evidence; or 'hardened' – There's no way I'll believe this whatever facts or evidence you show me.

Cynicism is the tendency to believe that people are motivated largely or solely by self-interest. The word also comes from the Greek meaning 'doglike' or 'churlish'. Notice that the definitions we've offered are generalisations. The author Robert Anton Wilson coined the useful term 'sombunall' meaning 'some but not all'. Keeping this in mind lessens the tendency to take a generalised or extreme view. So, sombunall people are motivated by self-interest. Introducing children to this idea helps them to take a more balanced view when confronted by general views or belief systems, especially 'hardened' or dogmatic ones. Note in this context that superstition has been described as a credulous belief in things that don't exist, but there is also 'negative superstition', which is an automatic disbelief in things that might or do exist (though such things might not yet have been proven).

Generalised views often take the form of 'laws' or rules. So for example Murphy's Law states that anything that can go wrong will go wrong. Parkinson's Law has it that work expands to fill the time available for its completion. Less well-known laws include Betteridge's Law, which states that any newspaper headline ending with a question mark can be answered with a 'no'. The SF writer Arthur C. Clarke proposed the law that when a distinguished but elderly scientist states that something is possible, he is almost certainly right. When he states that something is impossible, he is very probably wrong.

Activity: Show the class these supposed laws and ask children to consider how far they agree with them, noting any exceptions ...

If it tastes good, you can't have it. If it tastes bad, you'd better clear your plate.

The food that tastes the best is the unhealthiest.

Every time you come up with a good idea, you find that somebody else thought of it first.

Less is more.

Nothing ever gets built on time or on budget.

You can also highlight the points we've been making by showing the children some proverbs (from the Latin 'to put forth the word'). Highlight the notion of 'sombunall' and also ask children to come up with scenarios where the proverb applies, and to think of exceptions. Also remind the class that some of these proverbs are figurative. So –

A bad beginning makes a good ending.
A miss is as good as a mile.
Absence makes the heart grow fonder.
Clothes make the person.
Delays are dangerous.
Great minds think alike.
In for a penny, in for a pound.
There is never a rose without thorns.
Practice makes perfect.
What costs nothing is worth nothing.

Thinking Critically

Developing critical thinking skills in children helps to protect them from exaggerations, misinformation, fake news and so on. We'll touch on this again later in the book, but for now mention that thinking critically involves –

Checking information by looking at more than one source.
Questioning doubtful content.
Asking for further evidence.
Noting whether the author cites source material.

Some urban folktales serve the same function as many proverbs, by offering advice or snippets of wisdom. One tale cited by Jan Harold Brunvand in his 'Curses! Broiled Again!' is that of 'the unstealable car'. The story goes that a man who owned a very valuable vintage sports car was so worried about it being stolen following a recent spate of car thefts locally, that he had strong steel staples sunk into the concrete floor of his garage, to which he chained the car by its chassis. He also kept the car covered with a tarpaulin, taking the vehicle for a spin only on special occasions and when the weather was perfect. When he next decided to go for a drive, he pulled off the tarpaulin only to see that the car was now parked the other way round than usual, with its bonnet facing the garage door. He also found a note saying, 'From the car thieves. If we wanted it, we'd take it'.

What questions would the children ask Mr. Brunvand to check the truth of this story? What questions would they ask the car owner if they were able to speak to him?

Brunvand himself admits that the first part of the story is believable – maybe there are car owners who are that protective of their vehicles. However, his suspicions are aroused by the fact that, first, he was sent several versions of the tale from different parts of the U.S. all purporting to be true and, he reasons, would car thieves really go to all that trouble to make a point? Brunvand also points out that the story carries the cautionary message that no matter how we contrive to fool thieves, true professionals among them can easily outwit us.

Another folktale which we've found children enjoy concerns the terminally ill grandmother of a recently married young man. For many years, grandma had wanted to visit Paris and her dying wish was to do so now, before her time ran out. Since the young couple had themselves intended to holiday in France, they decided to make the old lady's wish come true. Because of her poor health, the couple chose to make the journey by car. They'd booked a hotel for two nights, Friday and Saturday, planning to return on the Sunday. However, after taking grandma on a wonderful tour of the city on Saturday, when they dropped by to check on her on the Sunday morning, they found that she'd died peacefully in her sleep. This caused a huge problem: sorting out the paperwork to have grandma's body brought home would take days, and the couple had work the next day. With this in mind, they decided on a plan. They bought a rug, rolled the old lady's body up in it, smuggled it out to their car when the hotel was quiet and strapped it to the roof rack. Then they set off for home. Luckily the rug wasn't checked at border control and they made good speed up the motorway, so much so that they decided to stop for a coffee before pressing on to Sheffield where they lived.

But imagine the couple's shock and horror when they discovered that the rug with grandma inside was no longer there on the car roof. The straps had worked loose and she was gone. Knowing they'd get into big trouble if they contacted the police, they continued on home and, over the following several days, kept a close eye on the news – but no report of anyone finding a body in a rolled up rug ever came to light, and the police never called on them. So what happened to the old lady, and why did the incident never hit the news? (By the way, this story is true because it was told to us by a close friend who lives next door to the young couple concerned [Polly and Wally Doodle], at 23 Condon Road in the Birley area of the city).

Urban folk tales can also serve to highlight people's anxieties and fears, which is why so many of them reflect items often in the news (though not in the case of the vanishing grandmother), such as scandals, kidnappings, disappearances, murders and natural disasters. In saying this, such stories don't belittle people's fears, but acknowledge them by acting as cautionary tales and/or to allow us to think, 'Thank goodness it was them and not me'.

Note that scepticism and thinking critically are not the same as 'explaining away' something that doesn't fit a particular belief system. So with regard to Steve's experience on page 73, someone who doesn't believe in ghosts or the paranormal would perhaps explain it away as a trick of the light or a hallucination. An informative (sceptical) article on ghosts and 'seeing things' can be found at https://www.sciencenewsforstudents.org/article/science-ghosts.

* * *

3 Scientific Narratives

Overview

Science is one of the great human enterprises when it comes to exploring the universe and our place within it, along with philosophy and religion/theology (which, together with history, art, literature, performing arts and other areas with a cultural focus, make up the Humanities). Its application in the form of technology has transformed the world. The word science comes from the Latin meaning 'know', which is an interesting link with the etymology of narrative which means 'to come to know'. And while it's obvious that in the areas we've looked at so far; fictional stories, myths, etc., narratives form the template for these, science too has its underlying assumptions, values and systems of belief – its stories – that help to shape the way science proceeds and the way it's perceived by the general public. The author Chris Carter (Carter, 2012) proposes that knowledge is a belief that meets these criteria.
It is justified by the critical evaluation of evidence, therefore –

We have good reason(s) to think it is true and –
We have no good reason(s) to think it may *not* be true.

In effect Carter is implying, by calling knowledge a belief, and along with Postman and Weingartner (page 61), that facts are provisional and may, through further discoveries, be modified or discarded: science also doesn't necessarily proceed in an organised or linear way, as described in 'The Golem: what you should know about science' (Collins & Pinch, 2003). The fact that science is a human endeavour is highlighted by a remark made by Albert Einstein that, 'the sense experiences are the given subject matter. But the theory that shall interpret them is man-made … never completely final, always subject to question and doubt'.

The history of science is strewn with dozens of examples of new theories that have superseded older ones. Perhaps one of the most dramatic

Scientific Narratives 83

is the way that Newtonian physics 'works' when describing the effects of various forces on macroscopic objects, yet has been superseded at the atomic level by quantum mechanics and at velocities approaching the speed of light, where relativistic effects come into play. Incidentally, while quantum physics and relativity have both been supported by a wealth of observations and experiments, for the time being at least they remain incompatible. (Coincidentally, as we were revising this chapter we came across a BBC news article – https://www.bbc.co.uk/news/science-environment-60708711 – outlining the work of Prof Xavier Calmet of the University of Sussex and colleagues, who claim to have taken a step towards resolving the relativity-quantum paradox by developing the 'yes hair theorem'. Read more online.) One of the great aims of science is to formulate a Theory of Everything (TOE), also called the Grand Unified Theory (GUT), which aspires to be the ultimate explanation of why the universe is as it is.

Activity: Ask the children what they understand science to be about, so that you can prepare them (if you choose) to explore some of the links with narrative that we make in this chapter. Work with the class to list some of the branches of science and what they focus on. Take it further by researching the etymology of physics, chemistry, astronomy, etc.

(Referring back to 'The Golem', the authors point out in their Introduction that some people regard science as 'a crusading knight' battling against ignorance, on a quest to make the world a better place; while others see it as 'the enemy' that allows technological horrors into the world. These ideas are themselves narrative fragments, pointing towards more elaborate and extensive 'stories' related to people's perceptions of science and technology. Collins and Pinch assert that both views are wrong 'and dangerous'. They tell us that science is 'a golem', a creature from legend that can be clumsy and dangerous if not controlled. They also highlight the fact that science is a pursuit of human beings and, like all humans, scientists are fallible and can make mistakes. The authors ask us, in reading their book, to 'learn to love the bumbling giant [that is science] for what it is'.)

As an aside, on a smaller scale, the link between science and narrative is reflected in some book titles of popular science, such as; 'The Old Way; the story of the first people' by Elizabeth Marshall Thomas, 'Eureka: a book of scientific anecdotes' by Adrian Berry and 'The Apollo Story' by Peter Fairley.

Activity: Ask the children to think in general terms about science and make a list of what they regard to be its benefits and its disadvantages, perhaps prompted by Figure 3.1. Then, working in smaller groups, ask them to focus on one aspect of science/technology such as space travel,

Figure 3.1 Science for Good or Ill.

nuclear fission, the Internet, etc. and create a more specific list of benefits/advantages and disadvantages/dangers.

Activity: Ask children to describe a science lab (based, presumably largely, on what they've seen on TV and in films): in other words to identify the motifs of a science lab, including the scientists who work there. Follow up by showing images of science labs and compare these with the children's prior impressions.

Scientific Narratives 85

Activity: In Figure 3.2, which figure most closely conforms to the children's perception of a scientist, and why? Take it further: imagine that all of these people were scientists or inventors. What branch of science do you think they'd be working in and/or what kinds of things do you think they'd invent, and why?

Figure 3.2 Scientist Stereotypes.

Note: An academic article on children's perceptions of scientists can be found at https://www.hindawi.com/journals/edri/2019/6324704/, which reports that: 'Almost all studies confirmed that students have a stereotypical view of scientists where scientists are mainly represented as white males wearing lab coats, eyeglasses, with facial hair, and an eccentric appearance'.

Tellingly, keying 'scientists' into an online image search brings up pictures that almost always conform to the stereotype. Even searching for 'non-stereotypical images of scientists' brings up plenty of stereotypical images.

Activity: Show some examples of advertisements that use the motifs of science and scientists, including jargon – which may be scientific gobbledygook, see page 17 – that try and persuade us to buy the product. Take it further by checking these terms to see if they are accurate and true. Introduce the term 'buzzword' meaning a word or phrase that becomes fashionable for a time: 'scientific' jargon used in adverts are often buzzwords, which frequently derive from technical terms and in advertising are used to persuade or impress. Also note any vagueness such as 'clinical trials have shown ...', etc. Keying 'pseudoscience in advertising' will bring up plenty of examples.

Another important issue, explored by J. W. N. Sullivan in his book 'The Limitations of Science' (Sullivan, 1961), is that the core assumption within much of science is that 'the real may be identified with the quantitative'. In other words, what science regards as real are only those things that can be observed, measured and tested; a standpoint known as materialism – so from this perspective, Steve's 'llama experience' (page 73) would have to be explained away as a hallucination (or illusion or delusion, page 75), or a misperception caused, for instance, by a trick of the light.

The British biologist Peter Medawar in his 'The Limits of Science' (Medawar, 1986) notes that science is unable to answer what he calls 'childlike questions' such as; How did everything begin? What are we all here for? What is the point of living? Medawar asserts that science will never be able to answer such questions, referring to the philosopher Karl Popper who thought that these are the 'ultimate questions' arising out of what the philosopher Immanuel Kant called the 'restless endeavours' of humans to learn, know and understand at the deepest level. Mel Thompson in his 'Teach Yourself Philosophy of Science' (Thompson, 2006) asserts that within science there is no absolute certainty but only increasingly high degrees of probability requiring a 'leap of faith' based on the assumption that the universe is predictable. This is linked to what Popper has called 'promissory materialism'; the promise, as it were, that science based only on what can be observed, measured and tested will one day explain everything – back to TOE and GUT.

Activity: Mention the metaphors of science that we've looked at – the crusading knight, the enemy, the bumbling giant (Golem). Can children come up with any other metaphors that reflect how they perceive science generally (such as a light shining in the darkness, a two-edged sword, a magnifying glass, etc.)?

You may be wondering what any of this has got to do with teaching science in the classroom. We have a few points to make about this ...

What we've said so far relates to the process of scientific enquiry rather than to the 'facts' it uncovers; its content. We feel that giving children insight into the way science operates underpins the facts we teach them within the science curriculum. One aspect of this, as we've said, is that the overarching belief system, or paradigm – what the biologist Rupert Sheldrake calls the 'current consensus' – of science is materialistic, resting on the widespread belief that the whole of reality consists only of matter and energy.

We also contend, based on our experience in schools, that many children are intrigued by the 'childlike questions' mentioned by Popper.

Steve – Some years ago I was asked to run a number of creative writing sessions in a Nottingham school for a small group of 'challenging' Y7-Y9 pupils. One of the issues was that these children lacked self-esteem and the hope was that by giving them some 'how to' techniques to improve their writing, their self-confidence might be boosted. At the start of the first workshop, I introduced myself and happened to mention my interest in Astronomy. One of the Year Nine boys immediately jumped in with questions like, 'But why are the stars there? Why are any of *us* here? What does it all mean?' What struck me was the passion with which the boy asked these questions, his sheer longing to know. How I wish I could have spent an hour pondering these ideas with that student.

Some scientists might dismiss such questions as meaningless or answer them with responses like – The stars are just there. There's no meaning or purpose behind their existence. And we aren't here for any reason, since we are nothing but the result of blind evolution. In the end, life and existence are cosmic accidents ...

Such a standpoint isn't based on a platform of provable facts but assumptions arising out of what the philosopher Thomas Kuhn has termed a paradigm; a set of explanatory concepts (Kuhn, 1970). It's also worth noting that just because a scientist says something is true doesn't necessarily make it so, especially if he or she is expressing an opinion outside their area of expertise.

We think that children will benefit from understanding these points as part of the cultivation in them of a questioning and critical attitude.

Steve – At another school, I was invited to run some writing sessions with Year Six. I went to the classroom part-way through morning break to prepare my workshop. The class teacher was still there, tidying up after what had evidently been a science lesson, for on the whiteboard was written 'Light travels in straight lines'. We discussed this briefly, and what dismayed me as we talked was that none of the children had asked any questions about the statement – How do we know light travels in straight lines? Is that always true? What is light anyway? Why is it called light? The children had simply accepted the fact and copied it down in their notebooks. If curiosity forms one of the cornerstones of scientific enquiry, and of learning generally, then surely that attitude should be cultivated in the young at every opportunity.

Activity: Invite children to tell you what questions about life and the universe they would most like to ask, the things that puzzle or tantalise them the most. Show them a list of current mysteries that science has not yet resolved. For instance –

What makes us human?
What is consciousness?
Is time travel possible?
Can we make a machine that thinks like we do?
Are we more than just a bag of chemicals?
Do we really have free will?

For more, see Birch/Looi/Stuart, 2017; Brooks, 2010; Price, 2016. All three of these books feature other as yet unexplained phenomena that map out what can be called the frontiers of science.

On a lighter note, Richard Benson's delightful little book 'Everything You Think You Know Is Wrong' (Benson, 2018) throws up a raft of mistaken beliefs and inaccurate facts, some of which caught us out too. According to Benson –

You can't detox your body through juices, teas, diets and pills. Our kidneys, liver and lungs do a more than adequate job of getting rid of toxins.

Lemmings do not commit mass suicide by jumping off cliffs.

Lightning *can* strike more than once in the same place according to many documented cases.

Most body heat is not lost through the head; only around 10% according to Benson.

Earwigs will not crawl into your ears and lay eggs while you're asleep, for although the insect is nocturnal, it spends its nights feeding on other insects and plants. (Incidentally the earwig-in-the-ear story is one of the horrors that Jan Harold Brunvand recounts in his book of scary urban legends 'Be Afraid, Be Very Afraid' [Brunvand, 2004].)

We could go on, but that would only embarrass us more! (Though of course in the true spirit of scientific enquiry one would feel compelled to check Richard Benson's facts.)

In his book 'The Limitations of Scientific Truth', author Nigel Brush (Brush, 2005) points out that a popular model of science is that scientific truth is superior to all other forms of truth, a standpoint known as scientism. He goes on to list the premises on which this claim is made –

Scientific facts are completely objective.
Scientific methodology is totally rational.
Scientific truths are superior to religious or philosophical truths.
Scientific truths have generally disproved the existence of God.

With regard to the second point, author Philip Goldberg in 'The Intuitive Edge' (Goldberg, 1989) cites many cases where a scientific breakthrough came as a sudden flash of insight 'out of the blue', though often after the scientists concerned had been pondering the issue for a long time: as the chemist Louis Pasture said, 'Chance favours only the prepared mind' – see also Henri Poincare's model of the creative process on page 57.

The unquestioning acceptance of a set of beliefs in any field is known as dogma (interestingly, coming from the Greek meaning 'opinion') – what Postman and Weingartner have called 'a hardening of the categories' (page 61). Dogmatic thinking often involves the sometimes vitriolic rejection of contradictory ideas in the form of unyielding scepticism, and 'confirmation bias'[*], where only information that supports one's current beliefs is accepted. We feel that in developing children's awareness of narrative within the field of science, an appreciation of the successes of science needs to be cultivated along with a questioning attitude about its limitations and underlying assumptions.

One contemporary 'questioner of science' is the biologist Rupert Sheldrake, whose theories about life and evolution are seen as highly controversial by many mainstream scientists: when Sheldrake's book 'A New Science of Life' was published in 1981, the then editor of Nature magazine proclaimed that, 'This infuriating tract ... is the best candidate for burning there has been for many years'.

In 2012, Sheldrake published 'The Science Delusion' (the title being a counterpoint to the biologist Richard Dawkins's 'The God Delusion', an atheistic/materialistic polemic against religion). In his book, Sheldrake

---

[*] While writing the first draft of this section, we mistakenly wrote 'conformation' bias. Although this was a typo (or a Freudian slip?), it does reflect the fact that the temptation sometimes exists to go with the crowd and conform to generally held beliefs and opinions for fear of standing out or being part of a minority that's frowned upon.

takes ten core assumptions of science, flips them into questions and then examines each one, underpinned by the assertion that they can be investigated scientifically. One assumption is that nature is 'mechanical', i.e. that living things are analogous to machines. Sheldrake asks 'Is nature mechanical?' and goes on to explore this issue. His other chapter headings include; Are the laws of nature fixed? Is nature purposeless? Is all biological inheritance material? Are minds confined to brains?

Many of the concepts that Sheldrake discusses are likely to go beyond the understanding of most primary school children, but we mention him as an example of the questioning attitude that we have been advocating; an attitude that steers a healthy path between hardened dogmatism and gullibility. And although time is at a premium within a packed curriculum, we do recommend that at least on some occasions you encourage children to ask 'how do we know?'

Along with a healthy tendency to question, there comes a certain tolerance of alternative perspectives. However, author and philosopher Peter Vardy in his book 'What is Truth? (Vardy, 2003) warns of the danger of what he calls 'radical relativism', an emotional and philosophical standpoint that denies the existence of absolute truth, claiming that there is only truth to a particular individual, culture or time. This is to say that all 'truths' are equally valid. Vardy speaks out very strongly in favour of a curriculum that 'takes the search for truth seriously', asserting that unless there is a truth to be sought, the distinction between truth and untruth becomes meaningless, going on to say that in the absence of a search for truth, the most powerful influence on young people are the media and what Vardy calls 'the world of appearance'. He further argues that poets, artists and writers have sought truth and devoted their lives to it, pointing out the dangers of uncritical acceptance of the 'founding doctrines and documents of a tradition' (quoting history professor Felipe Fernandez-Armesto), i.e. the drift towards fundamentalism. We'll look at this subject again later in the context of fake news, post truth, misinformation, etc.

A useful article on 'the search for truth', relying heavily on the thoughts of the philosopher Karl Popper, can be found at https://www.themarginalian.org/2017/01/26/karl-popper-in-search-of-a-better-world-truth-certainty/.

Metaphors within Science

At its most basic, all language is representational – as the mathematician Alfred Korzybski said, 'the word is not the thing' in the same way that a map is not the territory and a menu is not a meal. But within that broad concept (as opposed to metaphors *for* Science – crusading knight, golem, etc.), when we look at the world of science, we find a raft of metaphors used in its popularisation to the general public, perhaps one of the most well-known being cells – and sometimes RNA and DNA – referred to as 'the building blocks of life'. Others include comparing an atom to the solar system (an outdated and misleading comparison), reading the book of nature, and comparing the way the molecules of gases interact with the collision of billiard balls. Rupert Sheldrake (in 'The Science Delusion') reinforces this insight by stating that 'the whole of science is suffused with ... metaphors' such as the laws of nature (when laws are made only by humans), the computer analogy when describing the human brain, and comparing the mind with software, or the ugly term 'wetware'. James Geary in 'I is an Other' (Geary, 2011 – A brilliant book on the pervasiveness of metaphors in our language, thinking and behaviour) points out that the advantage of metaphors is that they reframe abstract and/or complex ideas as concrete analogies that are more easily understood and which can give insights into the processes behind the theory. For instance, the idea of continental drift (the theory of plate tectonics) has been visualised as being like a rice pudding, with the Earth's crust as the skin sitting on top of the liquid-like 'pudding' underneath.

Such metaphors may be thought of as 'narrative fragments' pointing not just towards the 'story' of the universe but also to the story of the progress of science in understanding it, based on its underpinning set of assumptions.

Incidentally, the literary critic I. A. Richards defines metaphor as 'a shift, a carrying over of a word from its normal use to a new one'. The word itself derives from the Greek meta, 'across' and phor, 'to carry'.

Activity: Show the class an actual map and menu to help children to understand that 'the word is not the thing'. This concept is rather deeper and more subtle than saying that a metaphor is a 'shortened simile' that isn't literally true.

In summary, points to be made to the children are that –

Science proceeds in fits and starts (sometimes through intuitive breakthroughs) as much as by rationally based progressive methodologies.

Scientists are also human beings with their own values, beliefs and opinions. And, like any human being, scientists are fallible and can make mistakes.

Public understanding of science is fostered by the use of metaphors that point towards greater narratives about how the universe works.

Advertising often uses the (sometimes pseudo-) language of science as a persuasive tactic.

Nigel Brush in 'The Limitations of Scientific Truth' quotes biologist Stephen J. Gould who says that 'So much of science proceeds by telling stories ... We think we are reading nature by applying rules of logic and laws of matter to our observations. But we are often telling stories – in the good sense, but stories nevertheless'. This quote appears in a chapter called 'Science as Literature', where Brush highlights mythic/folkloric parallels between various branches of science and traditional tales.

One example of this is the story of human evolution, noting the work of anthropologist and science writer Misia Landau, who saw parallels between human evolution and the basic narrative template (page 18), having this insight while reading Propp's 'The Morphology of the Folktale' (page 13) viz. –

The hero is the ancestral primate.

The familiar world is the stable environment of Africa's rainforest.

The 'call to action' (facing the central problem) is climate change during the Pliocene period (5.33 to 2.8 million years ago).

The hero (protohumans) must embark on a hazardous journey by moving out of the trees and on to the ground.

The threshold guardian – the first major test for the hero – is the ongoing struggle to survive in this dangerous new environment.

The hero overcomes challenges through the development of bipedalism and greater intelligence.

Further challenges come in the form of a new series of events, such as climate change at the beginning of the Ice Age.

The hero triumphs over adversity through the development of modern civilisation.

From this insight, Landau draws four primary motifs (constituent features) that have been repeatedly used in the scientific literature to describe human evolution – the shift from the trees to the ground; the change of posture from walking on four limbs to balancing on two legs; the expansion of the brain with the attendant emergence of language; the rise of technology, morals and society. The story has been told in this way for decades. In 'Why Us? how science rediscovered the mystery of ourselves', James Le Fanu (2010) points out that Thomas Huxley's famous illustration of the skeletons of a gibbon, orangutan, chimpanzee, gorilla and human (readily found online) is an iconic[†] image that symbolises the narrative of the gradualist view of evolution that has influenced opinion for many decades and served as the template for the equally well-known image of gorilla, through primitive man to modern humans – key-in 'the ascent of man' to find it. These illustrations encapsulate one story – controversial to some – of how we came to evolve into our current form.

Activity: Use the narrative template on page 18 and show how the steps of human evolution map on to it. Take the activity further by making a

---

[†] From the Greek meaning likeness or image.

class display, asking the children to use pictures, their own drawings and pieces of research to tell the story of how we evolved.

Of course, referring back to the narrative template, there will always be 'villains' in the form of further challenges to the human race and, therefore, the need for humans to face those challenges to survive. (A writer friend of Steve's once said with utter conviction that 'technology has got us into this mess and technology will get us out of it'. The basis for an interesting discussion we think, see Figure 3.3.)

Activity: Checking the latest information is essential. Genome sequencing has shown that Neanderthals and humans mated for thousands of years. We all have some Neanderthal DNA in us – there's also an ongoing debate, given the mating scenario, about whether Neanderthals should or should not be regarded as a separate species from Homo sapiens. So in one sense Neanderthals are still part of the narrative of human evolution, although because they are extinct as a (sub)species in another context, they aren't, or are just considered a side branch. Portraying the Neanderthal as in the illustration as a type of 'throwback' is a kind of stereotyping: ask the children if this is how they perceive Neanderthals/'cavemen'? Note also that 'family tree', which includes Neanderthals, is another scientific metaphor.

Figure 3.3 The Narrative of Human Evolution.

Activity: Look at other topics in the science curriculum. Do any of these map on to the narrative template and/or feature some or all of the basic narrative elements (hero, villain, help, etc. page 8)? See also our discussion of Kieran Egan's ideas in his 'Teaching as Storytelling' on page 162.

Activity: Ask children to pinpoint some of the challenges facing modern civilisation – climate change, poverty, pollution, war, etc. and whether these also fit the narrative template.

Nigel Brush (page 89) quotes the astronomer and author Timothy Ferris who feels that a good scientist (or teacher or storyteller) always picks and chooses his or her facts to get certain points across. Consequently, a degree of distortion and oversimplification always occurs in any presentation. As far as children's schooling is concerned, we are all bound to follow the curriculum, which amounts to other people's picking and choosing of facts – an issue attacked with some passion in Postman and Weingartner's 'Teaching as a Subversive Activity'. As a side issue, Kieran Egan in his book 'Learning in Depth: A Simple Innovation That Can Transform Schooling' (Egan, 2011) advises that real education consists of general knowledge *and* detailed understanding. Based on this assertion, he suggests that as an addition to the curriculum (a big ask!), young children are presented with, or choose for themselves, one topic that they study from their first days in school through to graduation, with guidance from supervising teachers. Egan's claim is that studying in-depth in this way will allow students to know as much about their topic as almost anyone on earth. And depending on the topic, it will certainly reveal the narrative structure of its presentation. (Perhaps the closest we can come to this is to ask children to prepare short presentations on any hobbies they have.)

Steve – Facts chosen by a teacher-storyteller are often vivid particularities (page 26). My A-Level zoology teacher once described a sea anemone fixed to a rock at low tide as looking like 'a half sucked wine gum'. A geography teacher told our class on one occasion that chewing gum was originally made from chicle, a natural gum collected from several species of Mesoamerican trees. The joy with which she recounted this fact and the smile on her face constituted the emotional impact behind the vivid particularity of that moment. That's why I've remembered these snippets when I've forgotten so much else of the syllabus!

Falsifiability and Mumbo Jumbo

One of the features of scientific theories is their falsifiability, i.e. that any theory is only truly scientific if it can potentially be proven to be false. As such it is impossible to prove the truth of any hypothesis (a theory in the making) that contains a universal statement, one of the most well-known analogies being 'all crows are black'. While we can keep observing black crows for centuries, leading us to assume that the statement is correct with increasing degrees of probability, the next crow we see might be white, thus falsifying or disproving the theory. This leads Karl Popper to assert that every scientific statement must remain forever tentative.

An important point arising from this insight is that it allows us to separate out ideas and theories that are truly scientific from those that belong in the realm of pseudoscience. Pseudoscientific ideas/narratives are beliefs, theories or practices that often use the language of science, but which have no basis in scientific fact. Various websites list a number of pseudoscientific ideas such as –

Aliens visited Earth long ago and influenced the development of civilisation.
The Apollo moon landings were a hoax (we'll look at this later under conspiracy theories).
Astrology, the notion that people are affected by the position of stars and planets.
Cryptozoology, the belief that Bigfoot, the Yeti and Loch Ness Monster, etc. actually exist.

Steve – One of the first and still best known books to argue that aliens visited the Earth long ago is 'Chariots of the Gods' by Swiss author Erich von Daniken (von Daniken, 1971). I read it a couple of years after its publication in 1969 and believed every word of it, partly because of the influence on me of SF author Arthur C. Clarke's wonderful novel '2001: A Space Odyssey', published in 1968, and the film adaptation by director Stanley Kubrick that was released at around the same time. Von Daniken's claims filled me with wonder; the uplifting notion that humans are not alone in the universe and that far more advanced benign races care enough about us to help ensure our survival. It didn't take long though for other writers to dissect and debunk von Daniken's claims, notably Professor Ronald Story (apt surname!) in 'The Space Gods Revealed' (Story, 1977). Another issue relating to the notion of pseudoscience is that to some extent it depends on people's viewpoints and opinions. Hardened sceptics might claim that certain ideas and theories are pseudoscientific and dismiss them out of hand, even rejecting robust research in the field: the notion of telepathy being a case in point, some argue. (If you're interested in this debate, we recommend Chris Carter's 'Science and Psychic Phenomena' [Carter, 2012].)

Incidentally, a thorough and detailed discussion of falsifiability and how science works can be found in Carter, 2012, Chapter 15, 'The Nature of Science'.

The point to be made to children is that sometimes what looks scientific isn't always so, but that some people doubt or disbelieve ideas related to science while others don't. It's also worth noting Rupert Sheldrake's view that scientific dogmas create taboos, such that creative freedom to explore ideas and phenomena that clash with the accepted paradigm is constrained or frowned upon (see Fringe Science in the following section). One aim of developing narrative awareness, therefore, is not to dismiss ideas out of hand but rather, as we cultivate children's critical thinking and questioning skills, to make them less vulnerable to dubious (pseudo)scientific claims and their use, for example, in advertising – again, something we'll look at again later.

If you're interested in looking further into the topic of science versus pseudoscience, a useful article is to be found at https://blogs.scientificamerican.com/doing-good-science/drawing-the-line-between-science-and-pseudo-science/.https://examples.yourdictionary.com/examples-of-pseudoscience.html.
Author Mel Thompson in his book 'Teach Yourself Philosophy of Science' lists astrology and crystal therapy as examples of pseudoscience, which can be identified by the following indicators –

The use of terms that sound scientific but which are used incorrectly or in a misleading manner; so-called 'technobabble'.

Over-reliance on anecdotal rather than experimental evidence.

Extraordinary claims (from the perspective of mainstream science) in the absence of extraordinary evidence. This notion is based on a quote in 1979 by the sceptical astronomer Carl Sagan. He maintained that 'extraordinary claims require extraordinary evidence', though since he failed to define 'extraordinary' more precisely, this has led to some ambiguity in the use of his aphorism.

Lack of linkage to other research. Often pseudoscientific claims fail to connect with the current body of scientific knowledge.

Absence of peer review. Peer review is the process by which a researcher's methods and findings are checked by experts working in the same field.

Lack of self-correction. Pseudosciences often continue to exist and be promoted even when they have been disproven. Proponents of some pseudoscientific beliefs argue that since the idea has existed for thousands of years (such as astrology), it must be true. This is known as the 'argument from antiquity or tradition' – known in philosophy as *argumentum ad antiquitatem*. Drop this phrase into a conversation at your next cocktail party to impress your friends.

Again, these concepts might be too sophisticated for many children to understand: we offer them as a framework of ideas to inform your own methods of developing children's narrative awareness in the context of science.

The notion of pseudoscience is related to 'mumbo jumbo', which refers to meaningless, confusing or outrageous ideas (the term is linked to meaningless ritual), but ironically is also linked to scientific jargon, especially if it is used to bamboozle the general public or to create an air of expertise and authority (back to 'reversing the polarity of the neutron flow').

Activity: Ask children if they believe in supposedly pseudoscientific claims such as ghosts or UFOs, and why. The aim is neither to agree or disagree with any child's belief but to allow all of the children to hear the raft of reasons as to why their classmates believe or disbelieve in such things. So for instance a child might say he believes in ghosts because his dad saw one once or maybe it was the deputy headmistress of the school who did (page 58)! Prompt some further thinking by asking the child what would make him believe in the idea of ghosts more strongly – in other words, what further evidence would support what the father said.

(Incidentally, a UFO is not the same thing as a flying saucer. As you know, it stands for 'unidentified flying object'. So a UFO might be some perfectly natural or even commonplace phenomenon that cannot be explained by a given observer, though another more knowledgeable observer might recognise it for what it is. A useful book on this topic is 'The UFOs That Never Were' by renowned UFOlogist Jenny Randles, investigative journalist Dr David Clarke and author Andy Roberts. Further, UFOs are now increasingly known as Unexplained Aerial Phenomena, UAPs. The reasoning here is that 'unidentified' is a looser term than unexplained; 'flying'; implies purposeful movement through the sky; and 'object' suggests something physical. UAP thus implies further explanatory possibilities.)

As we've noted, robust critical thinking is a shield against gullibility. Gullible people are vulnerable to exploitation in various ways, not least in buying into advertising claims or belief systems that purport to be based on science, but which in truth are not. In their book 'Teaching as a Subversive Activity', authors Postman and Weingartner title their first chapter 'Crap Detecting', echoing author Nick Webb in his book 'The Dictionary of Political Bullshit' (Webb, 2010) who said that 'we must maintain our bullshit detectors in good nick'. As an aside, we would also recommend Webb's more wide ranging 'A Dictionary of Bullshit', Don Watson's 'Gobbledygook' and Ambrose Bierce's famous 'Devil's Dictionary', one of the most hilariously acerbic and cynical books we've ever come across.

Fringe Science

This is made up of 'fringe theories' that are collections of ideas departing significantly from mainstream ideas in science. According to Wikipedia (accessed January 2022), a fringe theory is not a majority view (presumably among scientists) nor that of a 'respected minority' – though this term is not further defined; respected by whom, for instance, and why? The article suggests that a fringe theory more closely resembles a hypothesis or guess or an 'uncertain idea'; a hypothesis being a tentative explanation that has not yet attained the more robust status of a theory. 'Hypothesis' incidentally comes from Ancient Greek terms meaning 'foundation' and 'placing under', while 'theory' again derives from the Greek for (rather confusingly) 'speculation, contemplation'.

Again be aware that what counts as 'fringe' is based upon the paradigm within which mainstream science currently exists. It's also worth noting that the *fringes* or frontiers of science (another metaphor) mean something rather different, and that they expand: various theories that were on the fringes of our previous understanding are now well established within the mainstream. These include; plate tectonics, the existence of Troy‡, heliocentrism (a sun-centred Solar System), Norse colonisation of the Americas, the germ theory of disease and the hybridisation of Neanderthals and Homo sapiens.

Hoaxes

A hoax is a kind of lie, a fraud designed to deceive. Hoaxes exist in science as in other spheres of human activity: looking at the relevant Wikipedia page will reveal a long list of examples, while author Richard Garrett's delightful little book 'Hoaxes and Swindles'§ (used copies still available online at the time of writing) recounts some famous dupes suitable for children to read. Hoaxes are perpetrated for any number of reasons, and word itself is thought to derive from 'hocus' as in hocus pocus – a trick or deception. A number of sources also link hoaxes to fake news and misinformation, topics we'll look at later in the book.

Scientists, being human and with reputations to uphold and tenures to protect, have been known to deliberately falsify the results of experiments in order to bolster a hypothesis or theory (falsification); to make up results (fabrication) and to use the ideas and work of another person

---

‡ An exciting account of Heinrich Schliemann's discovery of Troy, together with many other stories of archaeology, can be found in C. W. Ceram's 'Gods, Graves and Scholars' (Ceram, 1974).
§ Subtitled, amusingly, 'Piccolo True Adventures'.

without giving them due credit (plagiarism). An online search by keying in 'list of scientific misconduct incidents' will bring up many examples.

Complicating the issue is the fact that scientific experiments can be messy or inconclusive, as we've previously noted. Referring again to 'The Golem', authors Collins and Pinch (under the heading 'Science Education' towards the end of the book) cite the common classroom experiment of finding the boiling point of water ... The teacher asks students to insert a thermometer into a beaker of water that's being heated and to take a reading when the water is steadily boiling. The authors assert that almost no one will get 100°C 'unless they already know the answer and want to please the teacher'. Further, once the teacher has gathered the range of results, he or she may be tempted to explain away the discrepancies by offering various speculations. One student might have put his thermometer into a bubble of super-heated steam, thus accounting for a result above 100°C; another student might not have brought her water to the boil before taking a reading, so obtaining a lower figure and so on. Collins and Pinch call such explainings-away a 'renegotiation' amounting to 'social engineering' that maintains, in this case albeit in a minor way, the scientific orthodoxy; the expected result that past experiments have supposedly established. The same phenomenon can be found on a much larger scale in the way that scientists have standardised, for instance, the speed of light (a point Sheldrake takes up in 'The Science Delusion'), the length of a metre and the value of a kilogram and a volt. The authors go on to say that this amounts to 'a neat and tidy methodological myth', and that students would learn much about the sociology of science – the structures and processes within which science operates, as distinct from the facts or content of science – if they and their teacher were to ponder on the boiling water results and, even better, to look at further examples of scientific experiments where results have varied.

(As an aside, many hoaxes, including dangerous ones, proliferate online and are targeted at children. The same attitude of critical thinking – the same savviness – that we advocate throughout this book protects children in this context too: check 'facts', see if the information is real; investigate authenticity; look at other sources; think about whether or how the author is trying to persuade or influence; be sceptical.)

Finally, and returning to Vardy's 'Teach Yourself Philosophy of Science', he rightly says that 'There are many areas of life, such as religion and relationships, in which it is perfectly valid to have a commitment and a particular chosen view which is not dependent on science. We simply need to accept that such things are not scientific and we should not attempt to justify them on a scientific basis'; though perhaps it's worth keeping in mind the philosopher Hume's advice that we should proportion our belief to the evidence available, which packs into a nutshell many of the points we've been making.

Activity: The word evidence comes from the Latin *evidentia* meaning 'obvious to the eye or mind'. The implication here is that some things can be obvious to the mind that cannot be seen. If someone has religious beliefs, does that count as evidence that God exists? If some scientists believe that other universes exist, does that belief count as evidence that the multiverse is real?

* * *

4 Historical Narratives

What Evidence?

History is often told and taught through narratives. In 'The Myths of Reality' for example, author Simon Danser tells us that history is a version of events that people have decided to agree upon (or have accepted unthinkingly). Another facet of this issue is highlighted by Professor of Archaeology Ian Hodder who, quoted in Nigel Brush's 'The Limitations of Scientific Truth' (Brush, 2005), has it that the writing of history ceases to be a neutral endeavour. Instead, historians and archaeologists must consider the cultural context within which they are working, as well as the moral impact of the story they are creating. For instance, archaeologist Francis Pryor in his book 'Flag Fen: life and death of a prehistoric landscape' (Pryor, 2015, 4th edition) freely admits that he got some things wrong in the first edition, and that his interpretations have changed based on further discoveries.

The implication of this is that, as cultures change, history as perceived by that culture is fluid and can also change. Sometimes history has been decried as being just stories about the great deeds of important white men. In the past, there was some truth in this and in recent times historians have tried to rectify it by researching and celebrating the important roles that have been played by women and by representatives of minorities, as well as focusing on the lived experience of ordinary people. As Mark Turner tells is in 'The Literary Mind', 'To be a good historian … one must not only have an excellent control of the facts, but must also be able to weave the facts together into a meaningful, pleasing narrative'.

Who Tells the Poor Man's Story?

Certainly in centuries past the best chance of leaving some record of yourself was to be a person of importance. A king in a castle would have portraits made, his exploits recorded and his praises sung no matter how mediocre he was. No one would bother about the serf in his wattle and

Figure 4.1 Who Tells the Poor Man's Story?

daub hut, as suggested in Figure 4.1. Their lives have to be reconstructed by archaeologists based on the few traces that survive.

Activity: Ask the children what record there might be of a King's life and a poor man's life.

They will end up with a long list for one and very little for the other, so underscoring the point we make in the text.

The cartoon gives some ideas (paintings, written records, his clothes, his crown and sceptre) but there are others (stories, castles, a tomb and treasures from his palace) that they might brainstorm.

This will be in stark contrast to the poor man; all that might signify his existence would be his remains and perhaps some of his possessions (such as the metal plate) that may survive buried in the ground.

Similarly, civilisations such as the Vikings left no written records[*], so the only contemporary accounts we have are from some of their victims, such as the monks of Lindisfarne, who would understandably be a little biased against them.

The Attitudes of the Time

Historical narratives also reflect the attitudes of the time; from the Victorian era right on into the first half of the last century, many of the historical stories told were of Empire builders and it was taken for granted

---

[*] Although foreign chroniclers and writers have left records of their encounters with the Vikings.

that the British Empire was a good thing for everyone. Who wouldn't want their land claimed by outsiders?

Personal values change too. In the past white hunters, who visited far-flung places to slaughter large numbers of exotic animals for sport and exhibit their trophies in their homes, were regarded as brave and adventurous sportsmen by many in their day, whereas now, with efforts across the globe to save endangered species, attitudes generally are very different.

The Battle Narrative

Historical narratives are about more than self-justification though; they help create a sense of identity and shared purpose, people like to feel good about their history. Given time, nostalgia, selective memory and constant retelling, it is possible for a bloody battle to become a valiant triumph or a 'heroic defeat'. Psychotherapist Lee Wallas in 'Stories for the Third Ear' (Wallas, 1985) feels stories are the roots of all history as we know it, the oldest form of exchanging human knowledge and experience.

Another thing that influences a historical narrative is the obvious fact that we know how things turned out. The Norman Invasion of 1066 might have been seen as a pretty risky venture to people at the time, as indeed it was. Hindsight, we might think, is a great thing. However, author and broadcaster Nina Schick in 'Deep Fakes and the Infocalypse' warns us that 'synthetic media' can rewrite the historical record completely, as illustrated in Figure 4.2. We'll be looking at this again in the section on Narratives in the Media. The underlying point for the children is that the questioning/checking attitude we advocate throughout this book is as valuable when confronted with historical stories as it is in any other context where narrative is used to convey 'knowledge and experience'.

Activity (see Figure 4.2): How might the two soldiers feel in the immediate aftermath?

Years later, how might the young soldier describe his part in the battle to his sweetheart?

How do you think the other soldier describes the battle to the young child?

In old age, how is the story handed down to the soldiers grandchildren?

When the other survivor, now an old man, reminisces, how do you think he recalls the battle?

What do you think is the point of the final panel?

Steve – A delightful book I've come across is Richard Shenkman's 'Legends, Lies & Cherished Myths of World History' (Shenkman, 1993).

Figure 4.2 The Battle Narrative.

Figure 4.3 Evolving Stories.

While I think it's a little unfortunate that myths and legends are lumped together with lies as untrue stories, the book is an enjoyable compendium of historical accounts that are widely believed but no longer thought to be true. Shenkman's style is light, witty and sometimes a little controversial: the byline of his section on Britain, 'This Scepter'd Isle' is 'British history the way it should have been taught'; while a later section on famous historical figures is bylined, 'If you learned it at school, it can't be true'. Perhaps you'll be irked enough to track down Richard Shenkman's book and check out his version of historical narratives for yourself.

* * *

5 Narratives in the Media

Ways to Persuade

Jan Harold Brunvand in his book 'The Vanishing Hitchhiker' reinforces what we've said in earlier sections, that humans as a species feel the need to construct stories, a point echoed by Alex Evans in 'The Myth Gap', that we are 'creatures of story'. Perhaps rather cynically, Nick Webb in his 'Dictionary of Bullshit' ponders how we might assess a narrative. Craft? Nifty construction? Textual analysis? (We wonder if believability and persuasive power might also be factors). He goes on to wonder whether it matters if it's true or not, referencing his point in this instance to journalism and political rhetoric. We hope he's being ironic here, though it's certainly true that the media filters and packages news stories such that they become 'mini narratives' collectively offering viewers, readers and listeners a 'lensed' or 'processed' picture of what's happening in the world. Added to that is the bias to be found for example in newspapers that lean politically to the left or the right, or that claim to be unbiased. More subtly perhaps, the philosopher Alain De Botton, in 'The News: A User's Manual' (De Botton, 2014) cautions that journalists, in order to make a story as emotionally compelling as possible, not only pay close attention to the way an item is worded, but pick out 'animating details' and carefully control pace and structure. Some journalists, De Botton maintains, are not above adapting a fact, eliminating a point, compressing a quote or changing a date. If this be so, perhaps all of us, and not just children, should check the veracity of news items that are significant to us in some way, and not just merely of passing interest.

Ongoing situations can form the basis of news stories that appear for months or years; complex long-term narratives that might affect entire countries or even the whole world. As we write this book, the COVID-19 pandemic is coming to the end of its second year. Looked at 'narratively' we can say that the heroes are the medical teams in hospitals, the carers in care homes, the scientists who developed the vaccines and so on. The villain is the virus itself, while the problem is its spread and mutated variants. Partners could be counted as the support teams helping medical staff while 'help' is included in the above plus community volunteers supporting those who can't leave home, delivery drivers, shop workers, etc. The journey is the ongoing effort to develop further medical interventions, the drive to vaccinate people across the world and the knowledge gained about coronavirus and how the human race might deal with future pandemics. The object(ive) is to put an end to the threat of COVID-19, as far as this is possible. With regard to the narrative template (page 18), different countries are scattered along its double loop as their own stories of COVID unfold.

Activity: Without explaining the above to the children, ask them if they can see the pandemic narratively. Or (if hopefully this is ancient history to them) ask them to pick a current item in the news and identify heroes, villains and other basic narrative elements.

In his book 'The Persuaders', author James Garvey (Garvey, 2016) quotes the journalist Walter Lippman, who draws a distinction between the real world and what he calls 'the pictures in our heads', the simplifications we use to navigate a complicated world. Writing a century ago, Lippman felt that 'The real environment is altogether too big, too complex and too fleeting for direct acquaintance'. The point is even more relevant now a hundred years on, when the world is vastly more complex than it was in Lippman's time.

Garvey points out that the 'simpler models' we construct of reality are formed of stereotypes and generalisations. This idea touches upon an assertion within the eclectic field of Neuro-Linguistic Programming (NLP) that three, largely subconscious, mental processes human beings use to make sense of the world are deletion, distortion and generalisation. (While this claim seems reasonable to us, we must point out that many scientists feel there is no scientific evidence to support NLP, which uses outdated metaphors of how the brain works that are inconsistent with current neurological theory. Despite this, we can ponder on whether those mental processes are accurate in describing how we see the world subjectively.)

Activity: Introduce or revisit the concept of stereotypes with regard to people using Figure 5.1, pointing out that this is a subjective belief or judgement about someone or something based on what they look like on the outside. The term originally referred to a printing tool that produced identical copies. Show the class these characters and ask the children to decide 'what kind of people' they are, taking it further by separating out neutral observations from opinions and judgements. If stereotyping is evident, what questions would children ask of one or more of these characters to appreciate them more as unique individuals?

Narratives in the Media   109

Figure 5.1 Stereotypes.

Explain that stereotyping is a kind of generalisation and that while it's OK (though unoriginal) to use 'off the peg' characters in stories, in real life people are unique and much more complex in all kinds of ways. As Figure 5.2 tries to show, behind any person is their unseen world of what they think, how they feel, their relationships and history ... In other words, what we don't know about someone usually far outweighs what we know, or think we know.

Activity: Offer the class a vague sentence such as 'The boy was walking down the street' and ask the children to write a brief description of what they imagine. If necessary, give them some prompt words such

Figure 5.2 What We Don't Know.

as age, hair, clothes, weather and season. The aim of the activity is to highlight how interpretations of even ordinary simple sentences can vary enormously. The linguist Noam Chomsky made the distinction between deep structure and surface structure in our thinking and language; deep structure being the totality of concepts, ideas and feelings that accompany something imagined, while the surface structure is the language we use to express what we imagine. Point out to children that what they imagined is far more detailed than the simple 'The boy was walking down the street', for as well as all the details they thought about, memories and other associations that they didn't write down might have passed through their minds, or might indeed still lie at a subconscious level. One of Steve's tutors always preceded a lecture by saying, 'I am responsible for what I say, but not for what you hear', thereby recognising the deep structure/surface structure distinction.

Another factor that Garvey highlights to make us perceive and behave in a certain way, rather than making up our own minds, is 'social confirmation pressure', whereby each of us is more likely to do what other people do; to go along with the crowd and/or simply favour information that chimes with previously held beliefs and biases. He cites numerous situations that try to tweak or 'nudge' our behaviour in this way – movie posters quoting only favourable reviews, canned laughter being used in some sitcoms to prompt us to laugh, books trumpeted as 'Number One Bestseller' (note the capitals, and note the number of books that feature this phrase!), carefully arranged photo opportunities casting politicians in a favourable light and others. Garvey's point is that in no case does the poster or whatever tell you directly that the film or sitcom, etc. is any good; you are only shown what other people think and/or what some want you to think. So the underlying point to be made to children is that critical thinking and a questioning attitude cultivate independence of thought and judgement.

Although we've said elsewhere that 'the word is not the thing', the way an idea is phrased can have a powerful influence on how we perceive it ....

Activity: Split the class into working pairs. Give each pair one of these words – property, house, home – and ask children to write down what comes to mind, i.e. what association each word has for them. Discuss afterwards. Many children are likely to say that home sounds warmer, cosier and friendlier than property or house.

Activity: Highlight how easily bias or spin can creep into language by showing the class this example –

Around two hundred fans flocked to the music concert.
Less than two hundred people bothered to go to the music concert.

Note: The website https://www.thoughtco.com/what-is-biased-language offers a useful article on biased language in various fields and how it can be avoided.

Activity: Ask children to look at some takeaway menus. Can they spot any words or descriptions designed to make the dish appear more tempting? Glancing at our local Indian takeaway menu we found; tangy, specially prepared, succulent, luscious, fragrant, plentiful, cooked to chef's own special recipe, fresh, lightly spiced batter, served on a sizzling skillet, distinctive flavour, mouth-watering, popular, unique, tender, thick sauce, slightly sweet, chef's secret recipe, aromatic, exotic, true Indian ingredients, 'to give it that Exquisite Reputation' (yes the menu did use capitals).

Conversely, our local Chinese takeaway menu is much more down to earth; spicy, speciality and most recommended being the only tempters we could find. Ask children to pick a dish from such a menu; chicken and sweetcorn, roast pork with mushrooms, fried mixed vegetables or whatever and use some tempters from the Indian takeaway menu to make the dishes sound more enticing. Children can use their own adjectives as well, but point out that piling too many adjectives one on top of the other lessens their effect, and in writing more generally is considered bad style.

Activity: Split the children into small groups. Ask each group to write a short description of the school as though for prospective new parents and pupils. Make the description as 'tempting' as possible with words like exciting, friendly, enjoyable, vibrant, etc. There's an opportunity here to practise thesaurus use. (Hopefully the children won't tackle this task in a cynical way!)

Towards the end of his book, James Garvey comments on the questionable morality of targeting advertisements at children, calling this kind of manipulation 'a new wrong in the world', ushered in by recent insights and discoveries in psychology and linguistics. He cites philosopher Martha Nussbaum that one way of countering the trend is to teach critical thinking in schools and, further, that it should have a *central* place in schools and universities; if not a return to formal grammar, logic and rhetoric, then at least an emphasis on thinking clearly and well. Garvey makes this point in the context of highlighting the importance of teaching the skills of reasoned argument. He devotes much space to this, stressing that it acts as a counterbalance to the way in which persuasive tactics prey on people's emotions rather than offering reasons. He is also troubled by the possible linkages between emotional persuasion and the tendency of at least some people to react emotionally themselves in certain situations, with anger and aggression as a knee-jerk reflex. (Indeed, as we write this, we hear in the news of violent clashes between police and crowds opposed to the tightening of COVID restrictions in some areas, and of anti-vaccination protesters massing outside school gates. Doubtless when you read this other examples will be currently in the news.)

A related issue is that people in a crowd may act more radically since, among the many, individuals can 'become anonymous' and abrogate the sense of personal responsibility they might feel if they had to act alone or in a small group. Crowds are also more easily influenced en masse, again by rhetoric and emotional manipulation; issues explored in detail in books such as Elias Canetti's 'Crowds and Power' (Canetti, 1984), Charles Mackay's 'Extraordinary Popular Delusions and the Madness of Crowds' (Mackay, 1995) and Gustav le Bon's 'The Crowd' (le Bon, 1969 – the edition we used) – a book known to have been studied by Adolf Hitler.)

Activity: Point out to children that advertisements are 'mini narratives' or narrative fragments suggesting more complex portrayals, usually of desirable personas, scenarios and lifestyles. Highlight too that advertisements are designed above all to persuade us to buy things and that *every* aspect of an ad is created for this purpose. Then show the class a few advertisements – not necessarily ones targeted at youngsters – and ask if children can pick out some of the persuasive tactics being employed. Also ask them to think about what stories are being told or suggested in your examples.

If you do decide to show the class adverts targeted at children, asking them to look at *how* they are aiming to persuade will help to 'neutralise' the advertisements' effects. Children are likely to spot more obvious tactics such as the use of cartoon characters, music 'icons' and sports' personalities, but more subtle and sophisticated ploys are used across social media. Commonsensemedia.org (accessed January 2022) warns us that social media 'influencers' get paid for endorsing products, while children and teens are encouraged to sign up for mobile alerts to get the latest news about certain TV shows, as well as ads from the companies that have bought the children's information when they signed up. Other tactics include embedding advertisements in video games and 'data harvesting' based on children's online activity. Even downloading an app requires potential users to give out information that advertisers can use. And don't get us started on cookies!* According to commonsensemedia, making children 'ad savvy' goes a long way towards preventing them from being exploited by developing what psychologytoday.com calls a 'working defence system'.

---

* Many websites don't allow the visitor to turn off 'strictly necessary' or 'legitimate interest' cookies. On one website we visit often we counted around 77 cookies that are always on. Granted, the website does explain in detail why these cookies are deemed necessary, admitting that commercial advertising and 'advertiser microsites' help to generate income.

You might explain cookies to the children and ask whether or to what extent they are happy to have their browsing information harvested and passed on. Incidentally, 'cookie' comes from the older programming term 'magic cookie', which was a data package that kept data unchanged even after being sent and received a number of times. Apparently the 'magic' tag implies some obscure data 'known' only to the software and not to the user.

Activity: All of us, children included, 'absorb' the techniques advertisers use to tempt us to buy their products. Try the following technique to heighten children's awareness of persuasive tactics in advertising –

Play ads without sound so that attention is focused on the imagery; colours, characters, the visual story being told, etc.
Play adverts with sound only and ask children to imagine what visuals might accompany the audio.
Play the opening ten seconds of an advertisement and ask children to predict what the rest might be like.

Ask children to listen carefully to an advert (maybe more than once) and pick out key (i.e. persuasive) words and phrases. Or you can compile a list of such tempter words and ask children to tick them off as they listen to a sequence of advertisements.

Activity: Product placement is where companies pay to have their products featured in films and TV programmes, sometimes fleetingly and subtly, but the message may come across nonetheless. Ask children to be on the lookout for this when they next turn on the television or watch a DVD or streamed content. Alternatively, show the class age-appropriate product placement clips from films and TV series.

Activity: Showing appropriate adverts from past decades – many are available on YouTube – allows children to see how slick and sophisticated advertising has become since then. Some old adverts, being 'of their time', feature various 'isms' that are considered inappropriate and even offensive today. You can take the discussion further by asking if, in the children's opinion, it's right that such adverts can still be viewed or, since they might offend, whether they should be banned. This topic relates to the larger issue of historical revisionism, which is the reinterpretation of an historical account. Another angle on this is the wish to 'delete' certain historical figures or events. For instance, during the writing of this section, four members of the public – the Colston Four – were acquitted of criminal damage for taking part in the tearing-down of a bronze statue of the slave trader Edward Colston (1636–1721). Ask children if they approve of the Colston Four's actions. You may choose to tell the class that the Four were taking part in a Black Lives Matter protest at the time, and whether this alters any of the children's opinions. (Coincidentally, while drafting this section, we note in the news that the government has just issued 'political impartiality in schools' guidance. We also read some commentators' opinions that this amounts to telling teachers what children should think. Or the guidance may be seen as warning against prompting partisan political views to pupils: one article made specific reference to the Black Lives Matter movement. If you want a broader perspective on this issue, key 'Political impartiality in schools and Black Lives Matter' into your search engine. Incidentally, the https://www.twinkl.co.uk/ website offers a range of resources at KS2 level for making children more politically aware.)

Activity: While it's the case that history largely consists of people's subjective accounts of particular events or periods of time, would it be fair to say that deleting history, as in the case of Edward Colston, waters down the 'truth of history'? As a thought experiment, ask children to imagine that all records of the slave trade were erased across the world, so that future generations wouldn't know that slavery had happened. Would this be a 'good' thing or not, and why? (See also the section on historical narrative.)

Activity: Another point that James Garvey makes in 'The Persuaders' (which he subtitles 'the hidden industry that wants to change your mind') is that every feature of large supermarkets is designed to make shoppers spend time there and buy more. He points out for example that essentials like milk and bread are probably placed at the back of the store, forcing customers to walk past other products that they might be tempted to put in the basket, while flowers, fresh fruit and veg are likely to be arranged near the entrance to the shop to create a favourable first impression. Treats like sweets and snacks are placed close to the checkouts – sometimes at a child's eye level – so that people queuing to pay may be tempted to add some to their shop (the number of times we've done that ourselves!). Point these things out to the children and suggest that they notice the examples next time they go to the supermarket. Encourage them to practise the questioning attitude by wondering why other products are positioned where they are.

Activity: On a smaller scale, bring in product packages and ask children to notice the shape and colour of the containers, pointing out that these will have been carefully considered by a design team before manufacturing began. What 'mini story' is the package and its labelling trying to tell us?

The Issue of Truth

'What is truth?' is one of the big questions in philosophy, and while the notion of what constitutes truth in different contexts is still hotly discussed, it's surely not controversial to suggest that truth of itself is a 'good thing' ... Or is it?

Activity: Ask the class to discuss whether it's ever good or right to tell a lie or to withhold the truth. What about telling a 'white lie' (note the colour association) to avoid hurting someone's feelings?

Incidentally, according to the author James Geary, the word truth is distilled from Icelandic, Swedish, Anglo-Saxon and other non-English words meaning 'believed' rather than 'certain'.

A much larger issue is that of so-called 'post truth', where objective facts are considered to be less influential in shaping public opinion (in adverts and politics for example) and where appeals to emotion are used instead. In Matthew D'Ancona's book 'Post Truth: the new war on truth and how to fight back' (D'Ancona, 2017), the author explores what he believes to be the declining value of truth as society's 'reserve currency' and the 'infectious spread of pernicious relativism disguised as legitimate scepticism'. Thus a lie might be disguised as 'misspeaking', facts may become 'alternative facts', while truth might morph into 'my truth'. The philosopher Nietzsche depressingly said that there are no facts, only interpretations: D'Ancona adds to that by asserting that fake news stories *feel* true, that 'they resonate'. Picking up the point made earlier about rewriting history, George Orwell was concerned about this decades ago. D'Ancona tells us that Orwell acknowledged that there was nothing new in the notion of historical bias, but 'what is peculiar in our age is the abandonment of the idea that history *could* be truthfully written'. D'Ancona also notes what seems to be a growing suspicion of science in some quarters, citing as one example the sustained modern campaign against vaccination (another topic in the news as we write this section).

These are dark and troubled waters indeed and to be honest we wonder how much younger children should be exposed to such ideas at this stage of their education. In a book about narrative awareness, though, we feel that the subject should at least be touched upon.

Returning to James Garvey's 'The Persuaders', early on in the book he lists some of the persuasive tactics that are used to try and make people change their minds over a whole range of issues ...

Infoganda – This is a form of propaganda; information framed to try and make people feel in a certain way or believe certain things. According to Wikipedia, infoganda is presented as though it were purely informational and not designed to persuade.

Sock-puppeteering – an alternative online identity or account intended to deceive.

Decoy pricing – the pricing of commodities to try and force customer choice.

Viral marketing – promoting products across a range of social media platforms.

Astroturfing – disguising the sponsors of a message by framing it as though it came from unsolicited comments by members of the public, i.e. as though from grassroots contributors.

Newsjacking – creating a campaign around a major topic in the news.

Framing – presenting information in a way that is intended to influence how people interpret it.

Greenwashing – falsely branding something as eco-friendly.

Nudging – coaxing or gently encouraging.

Further on in Garvey's book, he itemises ways in which some people (he cites politicians in particular) fail to address the issue at hand by changing the subject, appealing to the emotions and offering personal anecdotes as evidence. In tandem with this Garvey says that when he's exposed to these tactics now the 'boomerang effect' kicks in, or as we might say 'the law of reverse effect'. Many children might be familiar with this: ask them how they are likely to act if they're told, for example, 'Do *not* open that box!' after the adult has left the room.

Conspiracy Theories

This takes the form of a belief that a secret or powerful organisation lies behind some otherwise unexplained event. David Aaronovitch in 'Voodoo Histories: how conspiracy theory has shaped modern history' (Aaronovitch, 2010) adds that a conspiracy theory is the attribution of secret actions that could be explained more reasonably in a less complicated way. This chimes with the scientific principle of Occam's (or Ockham's) Razor, named after the philosopher William of Occam (1285–1347), who stated in effect that the simplest explanation – the one containing the smallest number of assumptions – is usually the best or most likely one.

Many conspiracy theories exist, a lot of them political and most (in our opinion) not suitable for younger children to be told about – just key 'modern conspiracy theories' into a search engine and you'll see what we mean.

One conspiracy theory that we feel is appropriate to tell children about is the claim that the American Apollo moon landing programme of the late-1960s–early-1970s never happened; that America faked it to beat Russia in what was then known as the Space Race. The Russians had been the first to launch a satellite into orbit (Sputnik 1 in October

1957); the first to launch an animal into space (the dog Laika in Sputnik 2 in November 1957); the first country to launch a man into orbit (Yuri Gagarin in April 1961†); and the first to launch a woman into space (Valentina Tereshkova in June 1963). There was huge national pride involved in these achievements and great kudos to be gained by putting astronauts on the moon and bringing them safely back to the Earth. Incidentally, President John F. Kennedy's speech on May 25, 1961, pledging that the country should commit itself to land astronauts on the moon by the end of the decade is one of the most stirring we've ever heard: you can hear it online and even pull up websites that do a 'rhetorical analysis' of how he made his words so compelling. Kennedy was assassinated in Dallas, Texas, on November 22, 1963‡, so he never saw his dream fulfilled. The first humans to reach the moon were Neil Armstrong and Edwin 'Buzz' Aldrin on July 24, 1969. (Michael Collins, the third member of the crew, remained in lunar orbit.)

Steve – A good friend of mine is convinced that the CIA was behind Kennedy's killing. When I visited him some time ago, he showed me a documentary to that effect which was very persuasive and which, for a time, had me convinced.

Although the Apollo programme is ancient history to your pupils (and perhaps to you too, you young things!), telling them about some of the conspiracy claims and how they are refuted offers a rich example of critical thinking, including invoking Occam's Razor.

Looking at some of the facts of the matter – Billions of people around the world watched the launch of Apollo 11 long before computer-generated imagery (CGI) existed to create a realistic fake launch; the ghostly pictures of Armstrong and Aldrin walking on the moon; the abundance of film evidence; the moon rocks that were returned to Earth, which have been studied for decades by scientists across the world; and the fact that the Apollo spacecraft was tracked by many nations. Added to that, thousands of people gathered at the Cape to watch that and subsequent Apollo launches.

There's no doubt that the huge Saturn V rockets blasted off from Cape Canaveral in Florida. Is it remotely likely that the American Government would make such a massive investment and not 'go the extra mile' of actually attempting to put people on to the lunar surface? Most convincing of all is the fact that thousands of personnel were involved in the Apollo programme and it's hardly likely that all of them could have kept the Big Secret for so long. Furthermore, as the Apollo programme

---

† and ‡ Conspiracy theories exist around these also, with some people claiming that a Soviet cosmonaut had been sent into orbit before Gagarin and that Kennedy was killed by the Central Intelligence Agency (CIA) (this being one of a number of stories surrounding the President's death).

progressed, the public rapidly lost interest and viewer ratings dipped, yet a number of further colossally expensive missions were launched. The final moonshot was to have been Apollo 21, but in fact the last lunar mission was Apollo 17 (December 7–19, 1972). Surely the US Government would have saved hundreds of millions of dollars by terminating the programme before then, having already won its political victory with Apollo 11?

There are other, technical, points that refute the Apollo conspiracy theory. One conspiracy claim is that because the moon has virtually no atmosphere, the sky is always black but there are no stars to be seen in the photographs, therefore the pictures must be fabricated. The most obvious response to this is that the 'fakers' wouldn't be so stupid as to make such an elementary error in preparing the images. Philip Plait in his book 'Bad Astronomy' (Plait, 2002) explains that because sunlight is so strong on the moon's surface, causing dazzling glare from the astronauts' space suits and the lunar surface, camera settings needed to be adjusted to compensate for this, meaning that the stars were necessarily dimmed out. Conspiracists also point out that the shadows visible in the Apollo pictures are not parallel: if there was only one light source – the sun – then they would be; therefore the pictures were taken in a film studio with more than one light source. However, the non-parallel effect can easily be observed by anyone: go outside when the sun is low and casting long shadows and you'll see that they're not parallel.

Finally, one of the most famous Apollo 11 photographs shows Buzz Aldrin saluting the American flag, which appears to be waving in the wind, though as we've said the moon is virtually airless§. So the photo must have been faked on Earth. If you show this picture to the children, ask them to look along the top edge of the flag and they'll see that it's supported by a horizontal metal pole, while the wrinkles in the flag are not caused by the wind, but are there because the flag had been screwed up and packed away for four days en route to the moon.

Coincidentally, when we were putting the finishing touches to this chapter, author Andy Saunders brought out a stunning book called 'Apollo Remastered'. He was given access to archive NASA film from the Apollo missions and used the latest photographic technology to bring out much more detail in the images. Such enhancement would surely have picked up at least some clues if the photographs were faked. Besides this, some of the pictures are huge panoramas of the lunar

---

§ The NASA website points out that the moon's very scanty atmosphere consists of some unusual gases, including sodium or potassium, that are not found in the atmospheres of Earth, Venus or Mars; but that for most practical purposes, the moon is considered to be surrounded by vacuum.

surface, sometimes with the Lunar Module standing there tiny on the skyline. Would NASA really go to the trouble of constructing such extravagant staging? And if the panoramas were created photographically (pre-Photoshop, etc.), then Andy Saunders would undoubtedly have discovered that.

David Aaronovitch in 'Voodoo Histories' feels that the prevalence of belief in conspiracy theories reflects a fundamental human yearning for narrative. He says, 'We need story and may even be programmed to create it ... We build a fortress of positive information around our beliefs and we rarely step outside'. Critical thinking, being led by reasons rather than emotions; noticing the language and the persuasive techniques information may contain; questioning the evidence; being open-mindedly sceptical – these again are the essential tools to cultivate in children to prevent them from being trapped in fortresses (note the metaphor) of false information that support unfounded and misguided beliefs. Don Watson in 'Gobbledygook' sums it up nicely when he writes, 'When words are suspicious, go after them ... Go after the meaning of the words'.

Clarity of Language

The other side of Watson's coin is his assertion that to communicate effectively is to convey information accurately and precisely. However, we often find examples of so-called inflated language and 'doublespeak', a term coined by George Orwell in his dystopian novel '1984'; deliberately euphemistic, ambiguous or obscure language (Oxford Languages). For example, a pharmaceutical company may admit that one of its products 'might cause some minor side effects' when the truth could be that it increases the risk of heart attack. (That said, guidance sheets that come with medicines often list at scary length possible side effects. We've stopped reading them!)

The word euphemism derives from the Greek meaning 'sounding well'. It's a technique for toning down or blurring ideas that might otherwise be deemed too harsh or offensive. So instead of telling friends that our great Aunt Edna has died, we might say that she's passed on. Other examples are –

He's been let go – he was fired.
The company downsized – some of the staff lost their jobs.
Setting out on a journey of self-discovery – jobless.
Enjoys shopping – chronic overspending.
Temporarily financially embarrassed – broke or in debt.
Golden years – old (we know how that feels!).
Well nourished – overweight.

And in education, how often have we come across late bloomers, interesting characters, self-willed pupils, 'bold' children and even challenging ones?

Steve – An R.E. teacher I once worked with wrote on every pupil report sent home to parents 'fairly fair' and nothing more. His aim was to get as many people as possible along to parents' evening so that he could speak 'accurately and precisely' about their children's behaviour and progress. He didn't want to be euphemistic in his writing, but also he didn't want to put frank or harsh remarks down on paper.

Activity: Show the class these euphemisms and ask the children to 'translate' them into plain, straightforward language –

1 He's a stranger to the truth.
2 She came into conflict with the law for removing someone's property.
3 Mr. Bowman is not as young as he was.
4 She never lets generosity get the better of her.
5 He does his best.

While we're on this subject, we want to mention weasel words and 'hurrah' words. Weasel words, a kind of euphemism, are used when someone wants to avoid being forthright, or where the speaker wants to create the impression of having given a direct answer, whereas in fact they've been inconclusive or vague. Individual weasel words include: a bit, basically, can, could, fairly, in a sense, many, may, might, moderately, most, often, probably, quite, relatively, seems, somewhat, usually, virtually.

Here are some longer examples –

1 Evidence shows that …
2 It's claimed that …
3 It stands to reason that …
4 Research tells us …
5 Many people believe that …
6 A recent study has found …
7 Award winning …
8 Critics of X have said …
9 Results indicate …
10 Mistakes were made, lessons were learned and procedures have been (or will be) put in place.

Activity: Get the children to challenge each of these phrases. For example, 'Evidence shows that …' What evidence? Who else or what other information can support that? Note too that such phrases are often to be found in advertisements and in statements made by 'spokespeople' on behalf of politicians.

Nick Webb in 'The Dictionary of Bullshit' defines hurrah words as those terms that are so popular or sacrosanct that it's difficult to criticise them, words such as: democracy, life, diversity, liberty, choice, freedom, rights, God, family and equality. Note how these crop up in politics and mission statements.

Something else that often gets in the way of accurate and precise language is the cliché, an overused and tired idea that indicates an absence of original thought. Many clichés are generalisations, while some purport to give advice such as; don't judge a book by its cover, every cloud has a silver lining, what doesn't kill you makes you stronger and the grass is always greener on the other side.

Steve – One of the most sickly-sweet clichés I've ever come across is, 'Aim for the moon. Even if you miss you'll land amongst the stars'. This optimistic bit of advice came up once during a writing workshop I was running with a Year Six class, the topic being clear and precise language. One boy, clearly too cynical for his age, responded with, 'Or you might crash land on the moon, or fall back to Earth and burn up in the atmosphere or get sucked into the sun'.

The unthinking use of cliché indicates lazy writing or, less harshly, that the writer was under pressure of time to think of more original sentences. How often, for example, have you come across 'pitch black nights' and 'howling winds' in children's writing? When we encounter these phrases, we ask the children what 'pitch' refers to (hardly any of them know), and ask them in their imaginations to hear wolves howling and then the sound the wind made as they wrote about it, and compare them. Of course, we wouldn't expect children to stop and think every time they were tempted to use a cliché: clichés are a useful shorthand and, perhaps more to the point, if children are 'going with the flow' of their writing, we wouldn't want to dampen their enthusiasm by them interrupting themselves umpteen times to rethink their clichés.

Incidentally, and returning to George Orwell, his guidelines for writing clearly and precisely are –

Never use a metaphor, simile or other figure of speech which you are used to seeing in print.
Never use a long word where a short one will do.
If it is possible to cut a word out, always cut it out.
Never use the passive voice where you can use the active.
Never use a foreign phrase, a scientific word or a jargon word if you can think of an everyday English equivalent.
Break any of these rules sooner than say anything outright barbarous.

You can find out more in Orwell's essay 'Politics and the English Language', readily available online.

In the context of persuasive techniques in advertising, sharpen children's awareness of written, spoken and pictorial clichés. These might include happy smiling families, cute kittens, puppies, etc. celebrity endorsements (surely they actually use the product?); thin, attractive, happy people eating chocolate for instance. This last example raises the issue of using unrealistic body images in advertising that can lead to an unhealthy mindset of comparison and dissatisfaction with one's own physical appearance. Many advertisements are slick and sophisticated mini-narratives that children – and adults – can buy into, sometimes with less-than-fortunate outcomes. Quoting Don Watson in 'Gobbledygook' again, he asserts that clichés are 'myths of language', here using the word to mean something untrue or misleading. He goes on to say that cliché-as-myth simplifies and provides meaning without the need of reason, which is why marketing and advertising use them so extensively; 'They stifle doubt and provide relaxation and comfort'.

Having said (ranted about?) all of this, we learn from the website https://theartofeducation.edu/ that clichés, notably visual ones, can be useful in the classroom. In terms of children's development, cliché helps to form a sense of understanding and camaraderie. Artwork featuring hearts for example conveys associations of love, while a smiley face signifies happiness. (We've also been in classrooms where uplifting, inspirational posters are on display – including 'Aim for the moon…') Thus, the article's authors recommend being tolerant of children's written clichés and those they use in their artwork, as they evolve towards more sophisticated and individual levels of communication.

Returning to conspiracy theories, we can argue that they are 'myths of the modern age', using the word myth in this context to mean something that's untrue. Philip Plait in 'Bad Astronomy' lists several criteria of truthfulness that he uses to support what he believes. In terms of conspiracy theories, there may be plenty of what believers term evidence but, to use Plait's term, this is 'written on tissue paper'. Examination of such evidence is likely to show that it is 'flimsy, fragile, and sometimes even fabricated', often relying on hearsay, second-hand information, bad statistics and non-reproducible events – the very antithesis of what constitutes a robust theory in science.

And yet there is a certain tension here and even a degree of inevitability in the appearance of conspiracy theories. Alex Evans in 'The Myth Gap', echoing Joseph Campbell and George Lucas (page 55), feels that today we *need* new myths (this time using the word to mean moral templates and narratives that help to guide us through life, or explanations that ease the tension or frustration of not knowing), noting that a new 'movement' is the flame that arises from the spark of a really resonant story; and many conspiracy theories would fit that description. The theory that the CIA was behind President Kennedy's assassination frames the CIA as the villains of the piece, while the climate movement casts exploitative rogue companies in that role. However, Evans highlights that the danger with such 'enemy narratives' is that they can polarise opinion, often in a political context; and as we've seen, such polarisation is more likely to be based on appeals to the emotions rather than reasoning and the kind of robust evidence that Philip Plait recommends.

In the News

The news presents a tiny snapshot of what's going on in the world: even searching such an extensive website as the BBC means that only a small fraction of what's in the news can be explored (time constraints in our busy lives being another limiting factor). News stories, particularly in written form, are small narratives that are structured around a headline, an opening paragraph, the body of the article and often a quote which usually expresses an opinion, notes Don Watson in 'Gobbledygook'.

Activity: Ask children to look at newspaper articles and/or stories on the TV news to look out for this narrative structure. It's not necessary to read the newspaper stories, but just to note the way they are constructed.

Activity: List the names of some newspapers – The Sun, The Mirror, the Mail and so on and ask children what 'message' or associations these titles convey. Some newspapers also feature logos near the name (logo from the Greek for 'word, reason, discourse'). The UK Daily Express for instance features a crusading knight – a heroic symbol: again ask children to think about what messages these logos wish to communicate.

Activity: Split the class into pairs or small groups and ask them to come up with a name and logo for a newspaper of their own, together with the reasoning behind their choice.

In 'Tales, Rumors and Gossip' (American publication), author Gail de Vos explores the use of urban legends presented as true stories within the media, more usually in 'soft' news items and the sensationalist press. De Vos early on makes a distinction between soft news and hard news that purports to be more objective. She tells us that contemporary legends have an ongoing appeal within Western society, and that certain sections of the mass media delight in communicating the drama, the warnings and the humour of such tales, which are more likely to be found at the tabloid newspaper end of the scale than in the broadsheets. (You might ask children to research the physical difference between 'tabloid' and 'broadsheet' papers to explain these labels.)

Activity: Perhaps you'd prefer to choose one or more news items that you suspect count as contemporary legends rather than true stories (so that children don't come into contact with any inappropriate material). Show your selection to the class. What indications are there that the stories count as urban legends and/or what questions can the children come up with to test the veracity of the tales?

As well as 'soft' news where urban legends might appear, and hard news stories about the day's major events that aim to be factual in content, de Vos also mentions –

Feature stories that focus not so much on a particular event but are more broadly based, describing general patterns and ongoing situations.

Talk show news which, de Vos says is widely seen as pseudo-news and, in conversations between talk show host and guests, can also count as gossip and rumour.

Docudramas, although often based on hard news, their main aim is to provide entertainment. They tend to form a continuum from legitimate factual documentaries to features that shade towards the fictional.

Activity: Whether news is hard or soft, it is made more compelling if presented as a 'human interest' story, again one designed to have an emotional impact on the viewer, reader or listener. As you watch a news programme, note the narrative elements used in its construction – hero, villain, problem, help, etc. (page 8) – and the emotions the feature aims to evoke in viewer. You can run this as a class activity by accessing news suitable for children at https://www.bbc.co.uk/newsround.

Activity: Ask children to choose a local event; something that's happened at school or in the neighbourhood and write a short news article about it. Ask them to set it out in this way –

- Choose a short and snappy headline. You can leave out 'the', 'a', etc. Look at some actual newspaper headlines to get the idea.
- Sum up what the story is basically about in the first sentence.
- Write the report using the third person and the past tense.
- Remember to begin a new paragraph when you make a new point.
- Put any quotes in quotation marks and any directly spoken words (from a witness for instance) in speech marks.
- A picture with an explanatory caption can make a report more interesting.
- Any opinion usually goes at the end.
- Check that the report covers who, what, when, where and how.

Although news reports aim to convey information, Don Watson in 'Gobbledygook' asserts that while the news purports to tell us what's going on in the world, it tells us in much the same way that the word 'biscuits' written on a biscuit tin tells us about biscuits, i.e. that the information is minimal and a surface feature of the deeper story. In comparing these, Watson says that the news is little more than 'signage', a kind of simple labelling or tagging of what amounts to much more complex events; this coupled with the particular news items selected by the programme makers. This chimes with the notion of what we don't know or think we know about people we see on the street (page 109), but this time with regard to events on a global scale.

Despite Don Watson's reservations, the BBC, and presumably other news providers, offers a reality checking service – the website https://www.bbc.co.uk/bitesize/articles/zmknnrd explains more about this and features teacher resources for educating children about conspiracy theories and fake news with the aim of boosting their 'digital literacy'.

Another valuable resource in our opinion is 'Deep Fakes and the Infocalypse' by Nina Schick (2020). This book sets out to highlight 'the increasingly dangerous and untrustworthy information ecosystem in which we now live'. One topic she explores is how increasing computing power and the ready availability of sophisticated CGI software is making it ever more difficult to tell faked images from real ones. Schick offers several examples from the field of geopolitics, which secondary age students might benefit from learning about: perhaps children at Junior level can simply be made aware of the concept of deep fakes as an introduction to their digital literacy: Matthew D'Ancona in 'Post Truth' quotes Apple CEO (at the time of writing) Tim Cook who said in 2017 that fake news is 'killing people's minds' and that awareness of it needs to be 'ingrained in schools ... ingrained in the public'.

(Incidentally, Schick lists several dozen websites that include fact-checking organisations, disinformation detection and protection sites and social media analysis links.)

Activity: Before the age of CGI, a technique called stop-go animation, or stop motion animation, was used in movies. This involves manipulating plasticine models by tiny increments, taking a snapshot each time. When the film is run, the clay models appear to be moving. Typically, it took 24 frames to make one second's worth of film – we say 'took' but stop motion is still being used, for instance in movies such as Wallace and Gromit, Coraline, Chicken Run, Shaun the Sheep and others.

One of the giants of the stop motion technique (also called 'claymotion') was Ray Harryhausen, whose work through the 1950s, 1960s and into the 1970s, mainly in science fiction and fantasy adventure films, was revered – and still is – by thousands of genre fans. Many clips of Harryhausen's work can be found on YouTube. Show a selection of these to the class, together with clips from age-appropriate modern films that use CGI, so that children can see the amazing developments in computer technology. (Incidentally, we learned while researching this topic that stop motion apps are now readily available so that anyone can make their own 'claymotion' films!)

Steve – Some months ago I was intrigued to see a clip of how artificial intelligence (AI) technology was used to animate the face of the Mona Lisa such that she moved, smiled and spoke. This has stuck in my mind ever since. It's eerie and haunting footage. You can access the animation on YouTube, together with explanations of how the effect was achieved.

Activity: You might also choose to show the class deepfake images, again readily available online. The point of exploring these matters is not to alarm the children, but to raise their awareness that these, together with mis- and disinformation, are out there, to encourage them that seeing is not always believing and to check information; think critically and question. (Incidentally, misinformation is where the purveyor believes the information to be true, while disinformation is the deliberate attempt to deceive with false information.)

We'll end by quoting the American comedian George Carlin who said, 'Don't just teach your children to read. Teach them to question what they read. Teach them to question everything'.

* * *

6   Therapeutic Stories

Stories We Tell Ourselves

The greatest of all 'self-stories' is our own life story, the span from birth to death and what happens to us in between. However implicitly, we organise our experiences into chapters: our life involves a cast of characters whom we encounter in different settings; phases of our life have beginnings, middles and ends; we meet heroes and villains, struggle to resolve problems, face challenges and seek help; our weaknesses may be highlighted and our strengths tested by 'threshold guardians' (page 20); the whole of life is a journey and, in many cases, our objective is to live a happy, creative and fulfilling one.

Within the course of a lifetime, we tell ourselves many stories *about* ourselves, more or less explicitly; we spin yarns that we weave up into the fabric of our system of values, beliefs and our own sense of identity. In that sense our psyche is narratively based. Psychotherapist Kim Schneiderman puts this concisely and clearly in 'Step Out of Your Story' (Schneiderman, 2015) when she says, '(Our) personal myths help us to weave together disparate threads from the past, present, and anticipated future into a coherent and meaningful narrative that captures who we are and hope to become'.

A few points need to be made at the outset –

Some of the stories that exist in our minds, and that help to define us to ourselves, are laid down during childhood. As children we are in a sense at the mercy of adults; authority figures who potentially have a great influence over us. Also as children (and into adulthood) we might create self-stories without consciously knowing so, without thinking them through. As such, these narratives and narrative/mythic fragments exert an influence over us at a subconscious level …

Steve – I have been a practising hypnotherapist for over thirty years. A yet-to-be-published manuscript of mine is a collection of case studies I've called 'The Story Behind the Problem'. Often, a problem that someone brings to a hypnotherapist – maybe a phobia, a weight issue,

DOI: 10.4324/9781003409038-7

anxiety among many others – is the expressed behaviour behind which lies a narrative; one or more experiences that have not been consciously realised (made real through recall and understanding) and therefore represent 'unfinished business'. I could choose from dozens of tales, but the case I'll tell you about concerns Brian who came to see me to stop smoking.

A standard technique to achieve the state of relaxed alertness that is hypnosis is to ask the client to close their eyes and think of a pleasant place. I could see that Brian was doing this because of the smile on his face as he imagined his chosen location. But within a minute or so Brian's expression changed to one of surprise. Then he surprised *me* by opening his eyes and saying, 'Now I know why I used to smoke'. It pleased me that he was already using the past tense. This is the story he told me –

> 'When you asked me to think of a pleasant place I imagined a lake. I've always loved lakes and rivers and there I was on the shore. Then I realised I was having a memory of a holiday I had in the Great Lakes area in Canada. And then I began to make the connection with smoking. On the second day of my vacation I met a young woman at a bar. We got on well and I asked her if she'd like to come out with me tomorrow. I suggested a little boating trip on the lake and then a picnic. She was fine with that.
>
> 'Next morning I booked the rowboat and bought our picnic lunch. The lady turned up on time, I took off my jacket and away we went. After twenty minutes or so I needed a rest. I put up the oars and asked my companion if she'd pass my cigarettes and lighter from my jacket pocket. She took these out – and threw them overboard! Then she said, "I hate smoking. You're not smoking while you're going out with me!" My immediate thought was that this woman wasn't going to tell me how to live my own life.
>
> 'Needless to say the rest of the date didn't go very well after that. We parted company and I didn't see her again. In hypnosis just now, as that memory came to me, I realised that because of that experience, smoking came to symbolise my sense of independence and self-direction. But I became a slave to smoking. Choosing to be a non-smoker now reasserts my independence in life and I know that when the nicotine is flushed out of my system, I won't have any desire to smoke.'

Not all cases in hypnotherapy are so quickly resolved – and I deliberately use that word because it chimes with the resolution of a story; a 're-solution' or solving again of a problem. The problem in Brian's case was his need to feel in control of his own life. Because of his experience on the lake, smoking became a solution to that need, while his reasoning after he understood the story behind the problem led to a resolution of the issue, with not-smoking taking the place of smoking.

(As an exercise for yourself, do you think that Brian's story contains any other of the basic narrative elements – page 8?)

It has to be said that hypnotherapy, psychotherapy, counselling, life coaching, etc. are specialisms that require training and much reading around the subject. The aim of this chapter is to make the link between self-narratives and mental and emotional wellbeing, and to point the way towards further resources in case you wanted to research more deeply. However, we will offer a few simple techniques that you can try out yourself, and that you may wish to use with your pupils.

The ability to notice and direct one's own thoughts is called meta-cognition, 'thinking about thinking'. For a thorough exploration of how this can be developed in an educational setting, see our 'Visualising Literacy and How To Teach It: a guide to developing thinking skills, vocabulary and imagination for 9-12 year olds' (Bowkett & Hitchman, 2022). Developing metacognition in children brings many benefits, not least an increasing ability to deal with negative thoughts and their attendant emotions.

Visualising

Activity: A useful place to start is to use visualisation as a way of relaxing …

Body scan. Ask the children to let themselves settle on their chairs. They can keep their eyes open if they like. Get them to notice any obvious tension in their bodies – relax a furrowed brow, unclench a tightly clenched jaw, let the shoulders drop, relax stomach muscles. Then ask them to imagine a disk of soft white light hovering above their heads, as in Figure 6.1. Let the children then imagine slowly moving the disk down through their bodies, with the instruction that as it descends it will allow a sense of deep relaxation to spread through the body. Children need to do this slowly, taking up to a minute or so from head to toes. You can pace this by holding your hand at head height, then slowly lowering it such that as it reaches your thigh (assuming you're seated), it should coincide with the disk of light reaching floor level. The activity can be repeated a few more times for extra effect.

Take It Further: White light, blue light. Again with the children sitting physically relaxed, ask them to notice their own breathing, then to take three deep inhales and exhales before returning to their normal breathing rhythm. Now ask them to imagine that as they continue breathing

Figure 6.1 White Light.

normally, they inhale a refreshing, cleansing white light. Some children will visualise this clearly while others might struggle, in which case tell them just to 'pretend' that the light is there at each in-breath. Emphasise that each inhalation of white light not only relaxes the body more and more deeply, but brings extra energy and vitality. The technique is more effective if the children's breathing is synchronised, so again you might want to pace their breathing by raising and lowering your hand, each in-breath and out-breath taking a slow mental count of one-to-three. (Note if any child is uncomfortable with this slow pace, just tell her to return to her normal breathing rhythm and ignore your pacing.)

After between six and ten cycles of breath, suggest to the children that they can keep the white light going (they don't need to visualise it explicitly but can 'pretend' it's there), but to notice now that as they breathe out, a blue light leaves their bodies. This blue light takes away 'all the aches and pains, the stresses and strains of the day' (as we like to phrase it). Again, if any children report that they can't see the blue light, just tell them to pretend it's there. Take the class through six to ten breathing cycles, then ask the children to visualise the blue light *and* the white light – the refreshing and relaxing white light on the in breath, and the blue light on the exhale that takes away stresses and strains. Again, continue for six to ten cycles.

In our experience, this visualisation can be profoundly relaxing for some children and, with practice, many of them will come to be able to visualise the white and blue light very clearly. Another benefit is that by paying attention both to the light and their breathing, children's minds are temporarily taken away from any negative thoughts they might otherwise be having.

The still pond. This simply involves asking children to imagine that they are sitting peacefully on the edge of a still pond. It's a pleasant day, the air is warm and there's a gentle breeze. Suggest that as they imagine the pond, they will quite quickly become as settled and still as the unmoving water. Don't go into too much descriptive detail about the location: let children use their own imaginations. Note that if any child has unpleasant memories of ponds or water, allow him to choose his own tranquil place.

The helpful stream. The same caveat applies to this visualisation. Suggest to the children that they imagine themselves sitting on the bank of a gently flowing stream. They can have one or more friends with them, fictional or real. Ask them to imagine leaves fluttering down from trees overhanging the opposite bank. As they touch the water, the leaves are gently carried away. Suggest that the leaves are worries, concerns or negative thoughts and they're being washed away so that they won't be troubling any more. Mention too that children don't need to know what each leaf refers to – you don't want to bring back negative memories; in fact, if any child re-experiences a worry, get her to transform it into a leaf and throw it in the stream, then watch it disappear into the distance. As with all of these activities, practice will develop the children's skill and allow the visualisations to become increasingly vivid and effective.

Reframing

Change the person. Many of us take a first-person perspective when we rerun memories, experiencing past events looking out through our own eyes. This is fine if the memories are pleasant, but one way of helping to decouple a negative memory from its associated unpleasant feelings is to shift to a third person perspective, imagining that you're standing there watching yourself as the event unfolds; a technique known as a 'psychologically distant vantage point'. You can combine this with 'rewriting the script', deliberately changing what was said and done on that occasion in order to create in your mind a different and more useful positive outcome.

Steve – A well-known mental technique is to imagine anyone you're intimidated by wearing a clown outfit or even with no clothes on at all – not that we'd recommend suggesting this to the children! But you can allow them to rewrite a memory in their own way, which they can keep completely private if they wish. I have to confess that whenever the memory of a particular bully who plagued me at school comes to mind, I shrink him to bug size and squash him flat. His cronies on seeing this run away screaming. I've used the technique so many times with this memory that the bully instantly and automatically shrinks. Sometimes for amusement I change the story and zap him with insect spray, or have a seagull swoop down and eat him for lunch. Over time this has served to dampen unpleasant feelings as the original memory is replaced by my new, preferred, and I must say very satisfying scenario.

The change-the-story technique above is a kind of reframing, which means looking at a situation, a thought or a feeling from a different angle. Even a few carefully chosen words can have a positive effect …

Steve – Sometimes when I set a class a thinking/writing task, I'll have a child come up to me and say he can't do it. My reply is always, 'Well pretend you can and tell me when you've done it'. 'Pretend' means that the task in some sense isn't 'real' while 'when' is a presupposition of success: at some mental level, conscious or otherwise, the child registers my expectation of his inevitable achievement.

Another kind of reframe is to shift the child's mood. On another occasion when a child told me he couldn't tackle a writing task, I asked him why and he said, 'Because I'm thick'. (Where did he get that from?). I immediately replied with, 'Well pretend you're thin and show me when you've finished the story'. That made him grin; his anxiety vanished and without argument he went away and completed the task.

Even more far-reaching is the story told to me by my friend Frank who, when he was at school, was by his own admission lazy and disruptive. The only teacher he liked and didn't hassle was an old Geography master who was coming up for retirement. Frank told me that on the final day of his career, the teacher took him aside and said very earnestly, 'I'm expecting great things of you'. Then he walked away and Frank never saw him again. 'But those few words completely changed my outlook. I started behaving, I knuckled down to work and I did well'. Indeed he did. Now retired himself, Frank eventually became deputy head of a large secondary school.

Expectations, both of our own and those that other people have of us, can powerfully affect how our lives unfold. This has been termed the Pygmalion Effect and was thoroughly researched in an educational context by American psychologists Robert Rosenthal and Lenore Jacobson. Their findings were published in 'Pygmalion in the Classroom', a book that we think is well worth reading – see Bibliography.

Verbing. Grammatically, this is the process of turning a noun into a verb. For our purposes, it's the realisation that each of us *is* a process, an ever-evolving story. An unhealthy habit is when we label ourselves in a negative way, i.e. use nouns which are static rather than verbs which are dynamic; a kind of nominalisation. We get ourselves into a state, as it were – something static or stuck. So instead of saying 'I'm a pessimist', we can reframe that by thinking 'I'm doing pessimism at the moment'. This acknowledges the dynamic nature of the behaviour and also plants the suggestion that it's temporary; that the 'pessimism-ing' will come to an end. This idea is related to insights of the poet Gerard Manley Hopkins (page 49), who coined the terms 'inscape' and 'instress'; inscape being the intrinsic form of something, its unique essence, while instress refers to the expression of that uniqueness in the world. While these have been termed 'mystical' ideas, we feel that they carry great power. Recognising one's uniqueness can raise self-esteem, while exploring one's uniqueness together with reflection on 'What can I offer the world? What do I want to achieve in life?' can empower one's personal narrative and give life a sense of direction. The American architect and inventor Buckminster Fuller famously remarked, 'I live on Earth at present, and I don't know what I am. I know that I am not a category. I am not a thing – a noun. I seem to be a verb, an evolutionary process – an integral function of the Universe'. We find this hugely uplifting, since it links one's personal uniqueness and life story with the evolution of the entire cosmos (in a way, connecting both ends of the ladder to the moon, page 52).

Personifying emotions. One way of working through unwanted negative emotions and enhancing positive ones is to turn them into characters. These can be simply imagined, drawn, put into a story or envisaged in any way that's helpful. If the character is just imagined, have him/her/it just talk: this amounts to so-called stream-of-consciousness work, though if you consciously just 'let the movie run' without intervening, it's likely that subconscious insights will emerge that might help towards resolving the issue. If you want to use this activity with the children, it's best done one-to-one with you there to bring the child back to the here-and-now if he begins to get upset. Kim Schneiderman, mentioned earlier, suggests casting oneself as the 'protagonist' and having a dialogue with the emotion you want to resolve, or at least find out more about. The emotion doesn't need to be imagined as a character and the dialogue might be carried on mentally or written down, again with as little conscious interference as possible. Schneiderman suggests that useful questions for opening the dialogue include: where do you come from? Why do you continue to haunt me? What useful function might you be performing?

A variation of the technique is to have the child imagine herself as the hero (perhaps in the company of friends/partners), while the emotion is the 'villain'. Then, either use the reframe technique as previously explained or suggest to the child that she imagines the narrative template, places herself upon it, zooms along the double loop to her starting point, by which time the villain has been defeated and the problem has been resolved. There's no need for the child to imagine any scenarios or memories, but should visualise the double loop as vividly as possible.

Another way of dealing with unpleasant feelings is to use them as 'creative energy' to drive a piece of writing, artwork or whatever …

Steve – Many years ago, I was very angry with regard to my profession (something to do with rapidly increasing bureaucracy if I remember). I decided to write an adult horror novel (using a pseudonym so that children who knew of my work for young readers wouldn't know it was me if they happened across my adult book). The novel contained plenty of violence. My anger was the driving force behind the writing and the book emerged as though it was writing itself. By the time I'd finished, not only had my anger largely dissipated, but I'd made some life-changing decisions that, I'm pleased to say, have since worked out well. The novel writing is an example of what I call a 'good anger': over two thousand years ago, the Greek philosopher Aristotle said, 'Anybody can become angry, that is easy; but to be angry with the right person, and to the right degree, and at the right time, and for the right purpose, and in the right way – that is not within everybody's power and is not easy'. But because writing happens word-by-word, the author has time to work through the emotion, some of this taking place subconsciously. What this feels like is the emotion fading over time, 'all by itself', though conscious thoughts and decisions can help the process along.

Another and more subtle point is that all emotions convey information. So, sticking with anger, someone might consciously know the source of that emotion, i.e. can connect the feeling with specific memories; but the anger might also be 'free floating', which is to say that the person might be aware of the feeling but not know why it's there. In this case, the experiences that generate the anger will lie at a subconscious level and may need the help of a specialist to resolve.

Many other techniques for dealing with feelings and cultivating mental and emotional wellbeing can be found in 'Jumpstart! Wellbeing' (Bowkett & Hogston, 2017).

Inspiring Yourself

The word inspire comes from the Latin *inspiritus* and means 'to breathe into', deriving from the Greek, where it referred to a supernatural being imparting an idea or truth to somebody. When children ask 'where do you get your inspiration from?', we make the connection between inspiration and breathing, and go on to say that when you have the clear intention to be inspired, you 'breathe in experiences and breathe out ideas'. In other words, cultivating the creative attitude within oneself. This is best done by 'being nosy'; most importantly by noticing things and by asking questions (these also being important skills for thinking critically).

Incidentally, in Ancient Greek mythology, inspiration came from the Muses, inspirational goddesses of religion, science and the arts. The word museum derives from this and means 'the seat of the Muses'.

Activity: Introduce or revisit the activity on page 65, where we used motifs as symbols. Once you've done this, ask each child to draw a circle on a large sheet of paper. This represents the child's inner world of thoughts and feelings. Now ask the children to choose a range of items and to reflect on what they could symbolise in a positive way, choosing objects-as-symbols that can act as positive resources. So a cloud could symbolise the feeling of floating on air, or of freedom. A shield could represent protection. A box could symbolise a treasure chest of other positive resources that have not revealed themselves yet – in which case the child might have further insights over time as to what they are and how they can be useful. The circle can also contain favourite characters from stories the children have enjoyed, each character representing a raft of positive characteristics.

Take It Further: Whenever a child wants to access the resources, she can simply remember the contents of the circle. Another technique is to 'anchor' those positive resources; in other words, to create a mental and emotional link between the resources and some small object that can be carried around such as a small pebble, or with a physical act that can only be done deliberately – rubbing the thumb and little finger of your non-dominant hand is a common example. If a child wants to use an anchor, advise her either to use the thumb-little finger technique, or to choose the object before she starts filling in the circle. Each time she writes or draws an object, encourage her to evoke the feeling or idea it symbolises. So if a cloud represents feeling light and carefree, ask the child to remember a time when she felt like that and at the same time to hold or trigger the anchor. Each time she adds something to the circle, encourage her to experience the positive thoughts or feelings and to use the anchor. Each time she does this, the anchor will become stronger, i.e. the physical-mental-emotional bond will become more powerful. The only downside to this technique is if a child loses the object that is the anchor. To circumvent this, suggest to the class that if an anchor is lost, then by choosing a new one, all of the positive resources from the circle will be instantly transferred to it.

You can take the technique further by having a larger whole-class pebble. When children have felt a positive effect from their personal anchors, have them touch these pebbles to the class anchor. Thus, the positive resources of every child are 'copied over' into the larger pebble, while the accumulated positive feelings and meanings of the class anchor are copied over into each individual anchor. Children can thus further energise and empower their individual anchors in this way, and 'power-up' a new anchor if the original pebble is mislaid. If you are in any way sceptical about this idea, give it try – test it for yourself: it's no more outrageous than Edward de Bono's thinking hats technique, and is in no way mystical.

Take It Further: Create a whole-class circle, where, as illustrated in Figure 6.2, each child contributes something positive to it and explains what the word or picture represents – to that individual of course; other children can put their own interpretations on it. This reinforces the sense of community within the class and exposes each child to ideas and insights they might not otherwise have had. Ideally, the class circle will be a permanent or semi-permanent display.

Activity: Stepping into character. Most if not all children will have favourite characters from stories. Ask each child to imagine one. If that person or creature had inner resources represented symbolically in a circle like the one above, what would the circle contain? If the child then creates that 'character circle', have him place it on the floor and actually step into it, suggesting that as he does, he'll experience all of the positive thoughts and feelings that the circle encompasses.

Figure 6.2 Whole Class Circle.

A variation of the technique is that once the character circle has been created, encourage the child to write a story or extract in the first person, where he or she becomes the character. Suggest that at least some of the character's positive resources; bravery, kindness, quick-wittedness or whatever are woven into the tale.

Taking inspiration from favourite stories is in itself therapeutic, where some of the positive traits of certain characters can be assimilated into the reader's psyche; this in addition to any 'moral messages' a story might convey. However, some stories are deliberately written to resonate both consciously and subconsciously in a therapeutic way. Author and psychotherapist Lee Wallas calls such tales 'stories for the third ear', using that as the title of her book (Wallas, 1985). This is a collection of stories to be read to children in order to tackle specific issues and clinical dysfunctions. Another useful book we've come across is Margot Sunderland's 'Using Story Telling as a Therapeutic Tool with Children' (Sunderland, 2000), where guidance is given on learning storytelling techniques to engage with children in the context of telling 'healing tales', together with case studies featuring children's own stories.

All of these techniques use the 'power of pretend', utilising the children's imaginations underpinned by the fact that the mind and the body are inextricably interlinked; that our thoughts have a powerful influence on our feelings and behaviours.

We'll end this section by quoting the educationalist Margaret Meek from her book 'On Being Literate' where she says that 'the stories we read or tell ourselves are necessary for our mental health'. She goes on to reference the psychologist R. L. Gregory who asserts that 'it is living by fiction which makes the higher organisms special'.

* * *

7 Stories and Learning

Many educationalists will be familiar with progress in children's learning being compared to a journey, in its narrative sense of a transformative experience (page 10). In this section, we want to explore various ways in which the notion of story structure can be applied in different learning contexts, together with taking a look at what we feel to be useful concepts to help facilitate this.

Activity: Work with the children to link the idea of the 'learning journey' with the basic narrative elements – hero, villain, partner, etc. and/or the narrative template with its ups and downs leading to the hero 'bringing home the treasure'.

Bloom's Taxonomy of Thinking

This model of the way a person's thinking evolves was devised in the mid-1950s by the American educational psychologist Benjamin Bloom and has continued to influence curriculum development since then. The taxonomy moves from what Mel Rockett and Simon Percival in 'Thinking for Learning' (Rockett & Percival, 2002) call 'simple thinking' with little understanding to advanced thinking that reflects much greater or even complete understanding of a topic – although we would qualify this claim: the physicist Richard Feynman for example, once famously said, 'If you think you understand quantum mechanics, you don't understand quantum mechanics'. So sometimes, when is full understanding achieved? There's also the philosophical point as to whether 'knowing' things about a subject is the same as understanding that subject.

Steve – My understanding of numbers and mathematical processes is low. I can remember getting long division sums right in primary school, without having any idea of what I was doing! I just went through the motions. And would a person need to possess *all* current knowledge of a subject, and keep up with new developments, in order to have a complete understanding of it?)

That aside, according to Bloom, the development of understanding progresses through a number of stages, also known as 'cognitive domains' –

Knowledge – remembering something learned earlier.
Comprehension – a basic understanding of concepts and the ability to put them in your own words.
Application – the ability to use knowledge or a skill in a new context or situation.
Analysis – the ability to see relationships between ideas based on an understanding of their structure.
Evaluation – being able to form judgements based on clear criteria.
Synthesis/Creation – the ability to generate new ideas based on previously understood information.

Note that the taxonomy doesn't necessarily suggest a linear progression. Children may be thinking across several of the domains during a task. Also, the thinking process with regard to the model is cyclical, referring back to previous knowledge and experience in order to gain further knowledge and deepen understanding.

If we accept the taxonomy as a working model, then we can clearly see how it applies to understanding narrative at increasingly deeper levels; for instance, in fiction, where the ability to answer comprehension questions about a story can eventually lead to a child's ability to create new stories of her own. Further, increasingly deeper understanding of narrative in its broader sense will also help children to ask more pertinent questions and have more frequent insights across a range of subject areas. Note too, therefore, how the taxonomy encompasses both critical and creative thinking.

Here are some story-related activities that we hope clarify Bloom's ideas and help children to move from 'knowledge' towards 'synthesis'...

Knowledge

Tell us about a story that you've read, watched or listened to.
    List a story's main characters and describe them briefly.
    Explain what it is about the story that led you to like and enjoy it.

Comprehension

Think of some questions about a story that you and your classmates have read. Be prepared to answer your classmates' questions about the same story.

Application

Identify the theme(s) and motifs in a story you've enjoyed and explain these to the class.

Find another story that shares some of these themes and motifs, working with classmates if this helps.

Analysis

Find a story that you think is written well. List your reasons for this.

Ask classmates to make a list of book titles and decide which fictional genres they belong to.

Ask classmates to show you some cover blurbs. Decide which genres they belong to and the reasons behind your decision. Also decide if the blurb is effective – if it tempts you to read the book and why, or why not.

Ask your teacher to show you an urban folktale. What questions would you ask the teller and/or the characters in the story to test whether it's true or not? Is there anything in the story that makes you doubt that it's true?

Find a topic in science that you think has a narrative structure; one that tells some kind of story. Prepare a short presentation to offer to the class that explains this.

Evaluation

Find a published story that you think isn't very well written, or that you didn't much like, and list the reasons for your judgement. And/or choose a story that you think *is* well written and explain why you think this.

Synthesis

Write a story of your own, perhaps using some of the planning techniques from this book. You can use characters from stories you've enjoyed but don't copy the plots. Put the characters into new situations.

Each child will naturally perform to their current level of ability and understanding, though children of all abilities might well be able to think across the range of understandings in Bloom's model, especially given a supportive classroom ethos in which they'll feel happy to tackle the various tasks we've suggested.

Related Thinking Skills

Different ways of thinking can be explicitly taught. Here are some that cultivate aspects of effective learning (and see also page 164).

Facts and Opinions. Even though, philosophically and scientifically, facts are regarded as provisional, a common definition is that a fact is something known or proved to be true. This contrasts with an opinion (from the Latin to 'think' or 'believe'). Facts may be used to support opinions, but the two things are distinct.

Activity: Ask the children to create a short list of statements, some of which are facts and some of which are opinions. Swap lists and decide which are which, using the following criteria if necessary –

If the statement contains words like should, possibly, might, may and could, it is more likely to be an opinion (though children could also search for facts that contain such proviso words).

Is there evidence (experimental or otherwise) to support the statement? If there is, it's more likely to be a fact.

If the statement comes from or is verified by one or more reputable authorities, it is likely to be a fact. Note though that different experts can have different world views – see for instance the disagreement between scientists Rupert Sheldrake and Richard Dawkins (pages 87 and 89).

Does the statement relate to someone's feelings? This is trickier, because strength of feeling doesn't of itself point towards a statement being a fact. Although a little simplistic (and philosophically debatable), a fact is objective and relates to something really 'out there' – the moon orbits the Earth*. A feeling is subjective and a matter of personal opinion – the sight of the full moon always inspires me.

If the statement contains words such as are, does, has, was, were and is, it is more likely to be a fact. But beware – 'The Apollo moon landings were faked' – see page 116.

Reaching Conclusions

The word conclusion comes from Latin terms meaning 'to shut completely'; in other words, a decision has been made and the matter is closed. However, it's possible to jump to a conclusion based on faulty assumptions, evidence that's been misinterpreted or through filtered beliefs (confirmation bias, page 89). More robust conclusions are based on evidence that can be observed, linked perhaps to previous experiences.

Activity: Old Man Jones suspects that a group of friends called the Double Darers (characters from the story below) have been sneaking into his allotment to steal fruit. Here are the things he's based his conclusion on:

---

* Technically (and pedantically), both Earth and Moon orbit around a common centre of gravity, the barycentre, located within the body of the Earth. So is 'the moon orbits the Earth' a fact or a partial fact?

142 *Stories and Learning*

Which pieces of evidence would lead to a robust conclusion, and which pieces would lead to a shakier conclusion?

1. He's heard that the leader of the Double Darers, Nigel Lloyd, gets into trouble at school quite often.
2. The gap in the chain link fence around the allotment is bigger than when he last looked.
3. He noticed what he thought was raspberry juice on the T-shirt of one of the Double Darers when he spotted the boy on the High Street.
4. The Double Darer named Anthony Morris looks shifty.
5. He found trainer footprints in the soft soil near his gooseberry bushes.
6. Brian Roberts lives on the Southern Estate, which has a bad reputation.
7. The name of the group, 'Double Darers' says it all really!
8. He's seen kids running away from the allotment area before now.
9. Some branches on his plum trees are snapped and have no fruit on them.
10. He used to scrump fruit himself when he was a boy, so these kids must be doing it too, because children are all the same.

Activity: In Figure 7.1 are some of the contents of three families' recycling and rubbish bins. What conclusions do you draw about the families?

Figure 7.1 Contents of Bins.

Note that coming to a conclusion based on evidence and reasoning is also called inferring.

Relevant and Irrelevant Information

'Relevant' means something that's closely connected to whatever is being done or considered; something that's to the point.

Anna Williams is another character from the story 'Crossing the Line'. Her cat Leo has gone missing and she decides to print off some leaflets so that neighbours can look out for him. Look at the pieces of information below and decide which would be the most relevant to put on the leaflet.

a   How quickly Leo can run.
b   His favourite kind of food.
c   The fact he's a male cat.
d   The fact he's a tabby.
e   The size of the cat.
f   The fact that he purrs loudly.
g   Where Anna got Leo from.
h   The fact he's wearing a blue collar with a metal name tag.
i   The fact that he's frightened of loud noises.
j   The fact that he loves to fall asleep on Anna's lap when she's watching TV.

Activity: Imagine that you've saved up to buy a new or refurbished laptop (or smartphone, or game console). List the items of information that you consider to be the most relevant in helping you to make your choice. Afterwards, discuss your reasoning with your classmates.

Crossing the Line

Here's a short story with associated questions that touch on some of the points we've made about narrative fiction.

Note: The characters in the story are in a group called the Double Darers, who dare each other to do things. But whoever makes up the dare must do the dare too. If they don't do the dare, they're yellow belly chickens, and if you're a yellow belly chicken three times, you have to leave the group.

The Double Darers Are

Nigel Lloyd, the leader of the group. He's mischievous and has an elfin grin.

Kevin Howells. He's really shy but very intelligent and has a mop of curly hair.

Anna Williams, tall and thin with long dark hair. She's mature and sensible.

Anthony Morris. He's got really skinny legs but is the fastest runner in the school.

Brian Roberts, a big square-looking kid with a big square head. He's built like a wall and acts as bodyguard for the group.

Neil Butler. He's shaped like a peardrop.

Ben Bowman, the narrator of the story.

* * *

By late September, we knew there wouldn't be many more times we could meet in the clump of bushes up near the Lime Pools to discuss Friday's special dare. The weather had been brilliant over the past few weeks, but in recent days, the temperature had dropped and the forecast was for more cloud and maybe some rain by Wednesday.

Anyway, there we were huddled up in fleeces and jackets listening to the wind rustling round us through the leathery leaves of the rhododendron clump – but only the strongest gusts got through, and each time that happened I gave a little shiver and pulled my jacket sleeves down over my hands.

It was a ritual that we met here in our other super-secret headquarters (the main one being Nigel's Dad's garden shed) on a Monday evening after school, to discuss the special dare we would do on Friday evening to celebrate the start of the weekend. As part of the tradition, Nige would give each of us a chance to suggest something if we wanted to, though unless the dare was really unusual or exciting, we'd end up doing the one he'd thought of earlier.

'Ok, who's got an idea?' Nige was wearing the woolly hat his Mum had bought for him down the market on Saturday. It was bottle green and he said it made for good camouflage (though he'd cut off the bobble that had been on top: he said the Special Air Service (SAS) don't have bobbles on the tops of their hats because it made them look silly).

Anthony spoke up first. His face was a pale blob in the fading light, though as he talked a faint glint of light from somewhere twinkled on his glasses. 'How about we go up Clack Hill and knock on doors and run away?'

'That is *so* juvenile', Anna piped up before anyone else had the chance to say anything.

'Boring', Kev added. He had the usual crazy look in his eye and I guessed he'd thought of something more original.

Anthony's was a pretty naff idea, but even so Nige paid him the respect of considering it: he stroked his chin and pursed his lips, which he always did when he was thinking something through.

'Well'. He declared at last, 'there aren't many sidestreets off Clack Hill for us to escape if anyone gives chase. Anyway, we played knock down ginger a couple of weeks ago'.

'Yeah', muttered Kev, as though that had settled the matter. 'So how about we do the Great Removal Plan again?'

There was a slight intake of breath from a few of us. We had done the Great Removal Plan once before, in Year Six. Turning up at school very early, we went into Miss Brown's classroom and moved all the furniture out, putting tables and chairs all around the school – including at the far end of the playing field. The only trouble was Mr Griggs, the caretaker, had caught us. Not only were we made to carry everything back (fair enough I suppose), but we were also put on litter-picking patrol for the rest of the term *and* we were given extra homework through the summer holidays. Luckily Anna hadn't joined us at that time, so she was spared the tedium of the punishment.

So, fearful of more of the same, we all made disapproving grunts and murmurs until Nigel's final say, which was, 'Too risky Kev. Far too risky...'

Slightly miffed, Kev lifted what we called his 'Elvis eyebrow' (it was like the sneery Elvis lip, but done with his eyebrow – he can only do it with the left one) and muttered, 'I suppose you've got a better idea then?'

'Matter of fact I have. How about we go over to the allotments and pinch some fruit?'

Groans and grumbles followed. 'Talk about boring, Nige'. Anthony shook his head in disappointment, obviously expecting something a little more exciting or challenging from Our Leader.

Nige held up his hands to dampen down our reaction. 'Wait, I haven't finished yet. Do I ever let you down? What I was going to say was, how about we go over to the allotments and pinch some of Old Man Jones's fruit?'

Our reply was a long and terrified silence, until Neil realised he'd been holding his breath and now let it out in a long shuddering sigh.

'No way'. Kev sounded adamant.

'It's certain death, man', added Anthony. Even Brian, who was built like a wall and wasn't scared even of our arch enemy Stonehead Henderson, looked uneasy.

Fact was Old Man Jones was six feet five inches tall. He'd used to be a miner out Clayton way before the pit had closed down, but he'd had to retire due to ill health. His doctor must have said to him something like, 'Mr Jones, if you want to live longer you must get yourself plenty of fresh air and exercise'. So Old Man Jones had rented an allotment off the council and spent much of his time there.

Now whenever you caught sight of him, whether it was on a freezing winter morning or a baking hot summer afternoon, he'd always be wearing a great black coat that came down nearly to his ankles. And on his head he wore a floppy old felt hat and his long hair used to straggle out from underneath this hat. On his feet, he wore these huge pit-boots: he was allowed to keep them when he retired because they were too big for any of the other miners to wear. There were steel nails, or segs, on the soles of those boots, and when Old Man Jones went down the High Street, those segs would strike sparks off the pavement as he walked.

Not only that, but whenever you caught sight of him in his allotment, if he wasn't holding a shovel or rake or whatever, he'd be carrying a great big stick. Lots of the people up at the allotments used to have trouble with rats and mice nibbling away at the fruit and vegetables, but not Old Man Jones. If he saw a rat in his allotment, he'd go after it with this big stick. BANG! Flat rat. And people up the allotments used to have problems with cats and dogs digging up the seedlings and bushes and leaving little presents (poo). But not Old Man Jones. If he saw a cat in his allotment, he'd go after it with his big stick. BANG! Flat cat. And a lot of the people up the allotments used to have trouble with kids sneaking in to pinch fruit … (Flat brat.)

So when Nige said we should go and steal some of Old Man Jones's fruit, we said 'no way'.

Nige often had this little smile or smirk on his face – the kind of smile that can get you into trouble at school, even if you haven't done anything wrong. Well that smirk grew wider now until it became a great big grin. 'But I'm daring you', he said.

And it was Anthony Morris who opened his mouth and put his foot in it because without even thinking he replied, 'Well we're double daring you –' Then he gave a little squeak when he realised what he'd done. We'd been dared and we'd double-dared back, so now we all had to do the dare; it was a matter of honour.

Which was exactly what Nigel had planned.

He dug in his pocket and pulled out a piece of paper, which he unfolded to show us. Kev helpfully flipped on his phone flashlight so we could see better. We saw it was a carefully drawn plan of all the allotments.

'As you know, Old Man Jones grows the best fruit and vegetables in town, but his allotment is the best guarded …' Nige reminded us about the chain-link fence that Old Man Jones had put around his patch of land, with barbed wire coiled along the top of that. And any weak spots he'd reinforced with old doors and planks of wood and sheets of corrugated iron.

'But just here –' Nige pointed to a red cross that he'd marked on the drawing, 'just here the staples holding the chain-link fence have come loose. You're a big strong kid Brian. You can pull up that chain-link to make a hole big enough for us to scramble through. So –' Nige looked pleased with himself. 'That's where we'll go in. Oh yeah, and we'll meet here at six-twenty to make the raid at half past six'.

I understood Nigel's reasoning. By six-thirty, Old Man Jones would most likely have gone home for his tea, and after he'd finished, it would be too dark for him to bother coming back.

'So you'd better turn up', Nige emphasised, 'or else you'll be yellow belly chickens. Oh and one more thing – don't tell anybody. Because if Old Man Jones gets wind of what we're going to do, he'll be waiting for us. And he'll be carrying...'

He didn't need to finish, for we all had that image burned into our brains. Old Man Jones wielding his great big stick.

* * *

I don't know about you, but if I've got to do something I don't really want to do, I grow nervous. By Friday afternoon, I was a quivering jelly. I came home and asked Mum if I could go out with my mates.

'Well you've had nothing to eat', she said sternly. She was in one of her I-don't-want-people-saying-I'm-not-a-proper-mother moods. 'I'll make you some sandwiches and you can take them in a bag. I'll do your favourites, cheese and tomato sauce'.

Normally I like them with so much tomato sauce squirted on that when I bite into the bread the sauce oozes down your chin. But for some strange reason I wasn't hungry.

'And you haven't had a proper drink', Mum continued. 'I can do you some orange squash, you can take it in a bottle'.

'No thanks Mum'.

'Full of minerals and additives for growing bones'.

'Mum, I'm not hungry or thirsty thanks'.

'And I want you back before it gets dark'.

'OK Mum'.

'And go straight there, to wherever you're going, and come straight home before dark. No dawdling'.

'OK Mum'.

'And don't talk to strangers'.

'OK Mum'.

'And don't come back with your clothes in a mess like you did last week'.

'OK Mum'.

'Off you go and have fun then Ben'.

'Thanks Mum', I muttered, slouching out of the house.

* * *

To reach our Super Secret Headquarters from where I live, the quickest route is down Maple Street past Brian's house, along the main road, then across the road opposite the junior school. I made sure I was there in plenty of time, as were all the others except for Kev. In fact he didn't arrive until around six-twenty-five. He came running along the lane, up the path and then crashed in to our secret Headquarters looking wilder and more dishevelled than usual.

'It's all off!' he gasped before any of us could get a word in. 'Forget it. We can't raid Old Man Jones's allotment now or ever!'

'What's the matter Kev', Nigel piped up. 'You a yellow belly chicken or something?'

'You don't understand …' Kev fumbled in his jeans pocket and pulled out a piece of paper, which he unfolded to show us. We could see that it was a page from the local newspaper, the Kenniston Gazette. It's a page you find in local papers everywhere; the one that tells you about recent births and marriages. And deaths.

Kev flipped on his pocket torch and we all read the announcement, surrounded by a black border, that Old Man Jones had died.

We didn't quite know what to do or say. I think we felt embarrassed or even guilty that we had thought about taking his fruit. Nobody looked at anybody else for a while, though Nige was obviously giving the whole matter some serious thought (he was stroking his chin).

At last he said, 'Wait a minute. Old Man Jones lived by himself, he had no family. It'll be months before the council sorts out the paperwork to let someone else have his allotment and by that time the fruit will have rotted away into the ground. What a waste! But listen, if we go in there tonight and take some, when we eat that fruit we can think about Old Man Jones and honour his memory…'

And that was the argument Nigel used to persuade us to go ahead with the raid.

The first thing we did was to crawl through the long grass to the pond. We scooped some mud from the bottom of the pond and spread it over our faces like they do in the army for camouflage (though Nige said he was still in the SAS). But, poh, it didn't half smell! That was perhaps why we couldn't persuade Anna to put any on. 'It's just like makeup, only brown', Nige told her. Still no good.

Next, we put some twigs and leaves and stuff in our hair, like they do in the army (or SAS) for camouflage, then crawled round to the place that Nige had marked on his plan.

Sure enough, the staples holding the chain-link fence to the post had come loose. Brian tested the chain-link and was easily able to pull it up to make a gap big enough for us to crawl through.

We all fell silent, hunkered down in the shadows and the growing gloom. There was a green smell in the air. A green, sweet, incredibly tempting smell; of apples and plums, leaves, grass and rich, healthy soil.

The woodsmoke smell was there too like a delicate perfume. The whole world was sinking into darkness as the sky turned purple at the edges and deep, deep blue right above. One or two of the very brightest stars were already out and twinkling.

Then Nige went into sergeant-major mode. He snapped off a dried nettle and swished it up under his armpit like a swagger stick. 'Right men', he began stridently, 'we are about to embark on a dangerous mission into enemy territory. Check your watches!' His tongue stuck out as he did this – it always stuck out when he was concentrating. 'Check those watches men!'

Trouble was, Nige didn't have a watch; he'd lost it. But he'd drawn one on his wrist in pen. And the time always said half past three, which was when school finished. None of us had watches either, so we checked the time on our phones.

'OK men', he started up again. Anna interrupted.

'What about me?' she wondered.

'Well ...' You could tell he was struggling to think of a reply that wouldn't land him in trouble. After a few seconds he gave up. 'OK people, in a few moments we're embarking on a hazardous mission behind enemy lines. But before you follow me through –' He pointed. 'Look there'. We looked and could see that Old Man Jones had dug a border of loose crumbly soil all around the inside perimeter of his allotment. 'He's put shards of broken glass in there to keep out the cats and dogs. And enemy raiders. So watch you don't cut yourself when you go in ... Anna, would you be on allotment patrol please? If you spot anyone coming, give me a quick call on my mobile'. He made an adjustment. 'I'll set it to vibrate'.

'What if the person who comes along is camouflaged, like you are?' she asked, reasonably I thought.

'You'll be able to smell 'em', Nige shot back at once, as she walked away and blended into the gloom. He gave us each a Co-op carrier bag and told us what fruit we had to pinch. My job was to collect gooseberries. 'Brian', Nige intoned gravely, 'pull up the chain-link please'. Brian did so, making a gap big enough for us to crawl through.

He was our leader so he went first. Next Anthony, then Kev. Then it was Neil's turn. Because he was shaped like a peardrop he got stuck. So there was his big bum in front of me and me trying to push him through – 'Come on Neil, come on man. Come on!'

Eventually the others had to pull him bodily. He popped through like a cork out of a bottle. Last, it was my turn, with Brian staying outside continuing to hold up the chain-link fence.

Nige's voice dropped to a whisper. 'Right, this is an in-and-out sortie. We've got five minutes then we're gone'. He pointed to each of us, indicating which way we should go.

Then I watched my friends disappearing into the darkness.

I knew that the gooseberry bushes were at the far end of the allotment, so I started to make my way. The first thing I came to was a clump of blackcurrant bushes. Now I don't know about you, but I like blackcurrants and I thought, wouldn't it be great to pick a couple of those bunches of blackcurrants and ... But I didn't have time, so I walked round and carried on.

Next thing I came to was a great tangle of blackberry brambles. Now I don't know about you, but I like blackberries more than I like blackcurrants, and there were some lovely ripe blackberries on those brambles. I thought, wouldn't it be great to pick a big ripe blackberry and ... But I didn't have time, so I walked round and carried on.

A few moments later, just ahead in the gloom, I could make out a beautifully cultivated row of gooseberry bushes. Now I don't know about you, but I like gooseberries as much as I like blackberries and more than I like blackcurrants. Thing is, if you eat a gooseberry before it's ripe, it's hard and crunchy and so sour that it makes your face screw up and the little hairs on the outside prickle in your mouth. But when a gooseberry is ripe, it turns yellow; it's soft to the touch and the hairs fade away to nothing.

And there, just level with my eye, was a big, ripe, yellow gooseberry.

I thought to myself, before I pick any of these others, I'll eat that one and as I do I can think about Old Man Jones and honour his memory. So I reached out for the gooseberry ... But before my hand got to it, I heard a clinking sound nearby. I looked round to the left and saw, about six or seven feet away in the shadows, this small shed. It was Old Man Jones's tool shed. I thought, I know what's happened – now that the old man has gone, the rats and mice are coming back into his allotment. And I'll bet there's a rat in that shed. It's running along a shelf and knocked over one of the tools. That's what it'll be ...

I reached out for the gooseberry. But before I could touch that gooseberry, something else over to my left caught my attention. I looked and saw that a light had gone on in that shed. I thought, I know what's happened – that rat has knocked a torch that's rolled off the shelf and hit the ground, and it's come on by itself. That's what's happened ...

I reached out for the gooseberry. And as I touched it and felt the fruit wonderfully soft and ripe under my fingers, there came this creaking sound. I looked – and saw that the door of the shed was slowly swinging open. And there, silhouetted in the torchlight, was the huge figure of a man.

I could see the long black coat that came down nearly to his ankles. I could see his floppy old felt hat with his long hair sticking out underneath. And in his hand he carried the Great Big Stick. He knew there were kids in his allotment and he was on the lookout for us. I froze.

He stepped out of the shed: his boot struck a stone and a spark flashed in the darkness.

Then he saw me. He lifted the stick, loomed over me and yelled, 'Get out of my allotment!'

I did what any normal, human Double Darer would have done under the circumstances. I wet myself.

Then I ran. I ran faster than I had ever run before. The first obstacle I came to was that tangle of blackberry brambles. Did I bother to stop and go round? No, I jumped up, did a somersault, snatched a blackberry, came down on my feet and carried on running.

The next obstacle I came to were those blackcurrant bushes. Did I bother to stop and go round? No, I jumped even higher, did a double somersault, snatched two bunches of blackcurrants, jamming them in my mouth as I came down on my feet and carried on running.

I could see all of my friends running towards the same hole in the fence, and there on the other side was Brian, trembling because he could see what was coming after us.

The first one to reach the hole was Anthony, the fastest runner in the school. He hurled himself at the fence and – Weeeowww! Away he went into the distance.

Next was Nige. Although he was our leader he wasn't hanging around. He threw himself at the hole in the fence and – Vrrooom! Away he went into the darkness.

Next up was Kev. He'd been pinching plums nearby so he was close. He hurtled towards that hole and – Whoooosh! Away he went into the shadows.

Just before I reached the hole in the fence, who should beat me to it was Neil Butler, who was shaped like a peardrop. He flung himself at the hole in the fence and – Jonk! Got stuck.

So there was his big bum in front of me and me disco dancing in desperation behind him. 'Come on Neil! Come on man. Come on!!'

In the end, Brian got hold of him and pulled him through. Ripped his trousers off. Neil Butler ran all the way home in his Winnie-the-Pooh boxers!

Then even Brian's nerve broke. He let go of the chain-link, turned and ran away. And if you've ever seen a wall running, you'll have some idea of what he looked like.

I guessed that Anna too would have high-tailed it out of there, so I was all alone, by myself, with no one to help me.

I thought, no need to panic. All I have to do is get right low to the ground and squirm under that chain-link. But as I began to hunker down something slammed into my back and flung me to the floor. I thought, Old Man Jones has got me with his big stick and now he's going to beat me flat. I waited for the end to come ...

After some moments I craned my head round and saw what had happened. Because he couldn't actually catch me, he'd pulled a big clod of earth and grass out of the ground and hurled it at me. It had shattered on my back and the impact had thrown me to the ground.

I thought, he's done me a favour, because now all I need to do is wriggle underneath the fence and I'm free!

But as I scrambled through, I felt a horrible sharp tearing pain in my left leg. I knew what I'd done – I'd cut my leg open on a piece of that broken glass. Did I bother to have a little cry and dab at it with a hanky? No, I ran along the lane past the garages across the main road down Maple Street into Cross Street in through our front door and into our front room ...

I burst into our front room and there was my Dad in his favourite armchair reading the Daily Mirror. And there was Mum in her favourite armchair reading OK magazine. As they put their papers down I saw them starting to get cross, because my face was covered with mud, I had blackcurrant juice smeared round my mouth, I had leaves and twigs in my hair and my clothes were all grubby. Mum was just about to kick off on one when she noticed that my left trouser leg and shoe were covered in blood. So she dragged me up to the bathroom, where she whipped off my shoe and my sock. She cleaned off the blood with a hot flannel, got a big wodge of cotton wool and glugged on plenty of liquid antiseptic – slapped it on – Aggghhh! – made me cry. Then she bandaged up my leg ...

And then she kicked off.

We never found out how Old Man Jones had come to hear the news of our raid on his allotment. I guess one of the Double Darers (but not me) must have mentioned it to a friend, who'd mentioned it to a friend – and so the rumour had spread, as rumours tend to. And Old Man Jones had come to hear of it.

We reckoned he'd worked out his plan then gone down to the offices of the Kenniston Gazette and explained it to the editor, who had agreed. Old Man Jones had forged his own obituary and had it printed in the paper to fool us. Then he'd gone down to his allotment to wait. And I don't know how long he waited, but he certainly taught us the lesson of our lives – don't steal someone else's fruit.

And it's a lesson I'm not likely to forget, because for the rest of my life I'll carry that scar on my leg where I cut myself on that piece of broken glass.

* * *

Next evening there was a knock on the door. Mum told me to answer it. When I opened the door, I nearly wet myself again, because there stood Old Man Jones in his great black coat, his floppy felt hat with his hair straggling out underneath, and his huge pit boots ... But this time he wasn't carrying a big stick; rather, it was a brown paper bag, which he handed to me without a word, then he turned and walked away into the gathering darkness.

It wasn't until I went back into the front room where the light was on that I saw the bag was full of fruit. And it turned out that he'd gone round to every one of the Double Darers and given us each a bag of his fruit.

So the next morning, by mutual agreement, we didn't lie in. Rather, we got up early and went down to the allotments. And there, of course, we found Old Man Jones. And we apologised, and spent an hour helping him to clear his ground.

* * *

Activity: Some questions:

What theme does the title of the story suggest?
What are the main narrative elements in the story (perhaps not all of them are there): Hero, villain, problem, partner, help, knowledge and power, journey, object(ive) (page 8)?
How closely do you think the story maps on to the narrative template (page 18)?
Are there any ways in which the story resembles an urban folktale?
Are there any ways in which the story is like a parable?
How does the author use the time of the year and the time of day to create the atmosphere of the story?

The author tries to put some humour into the story (as an 'ingredient', page 15). Can you spot any examples of this?
Notice that the writer describes the Double Darers using only a couple of details, making use of similes and exaggeration (Neil was shaped like a peardrop and Brian was a big, square-looking kid with a big square head). Think of a new character for the Double Darers and use simile and/or exaggeration to briefly describe him or her.

Do you think it's wrong for the Double Darers to try and steal some of Old Man Jones's fruit? If yes, are you tempted to change your mind, given Nigel's argument that with Jones having supposedly died, all of his fruit will go to waste? If some of the fruit had seeded just outside the allotment boundary, would you still consider it to be Jones's? If yes, would it be stealing to take some? If some blackberry runners or branches of a gooseberry bush bearing fruit had grown through the gaps in the chain link fence, would it be wrong to take those particular pieces of fruit?

Do you think knocking on people's doors and running away is wrong? Give a reason for your opinion. If you do think it's wrong, is it wrong in the same way as stealing Jones's fruit is wrong? Is the Great Removal Plan wrong? Give a reason for your opinion. Is it wrong in the same way as the other examples of dares? Would you use terms other than 'wrong' in these cases?

Do you think there's a moral to the story? If so, what might it be?

How do you feel about the fact that Jones responded to what the Double Darers did by giving them some of his fruit? Would you respond in the same way? Are there any other situations where you think kindness is preferable to or more powerful than punishment?

More Thinking Skills

Activity: While Bloom's Taxonomy (page 138) organises various kinds of thinking into a hierarchy, thinking 'skills' can also be taught separately, and within the context of a story. Here are some examples (see also other thinking skills in the section on Scientific Narrative).

Noticing the Properties of Things; Attributing

Picking out the characteristics of something develops observational skills. It's also useful in writing, where some attributes can be selected to include and others discarded. Also, picking out attributes from an imagined object improves the ability to visualise.

Choose one of the fruits in Jones's allotment and list its attributes. Include parts, uses, size, colour, shape and other features such as smell, taste and texture.

The Double Darers sometimes meet in their Super Secret Headquarters that used to be Nigel's Dad's garden shed. Imagine what the Darers might have put in there and list some of them, including a couple of attributes for each thing you imagine, for example cushion – soft, colourful, square.

Noticing Similarities and Differences

Choose two of the fruits in the allotment and note down how they are similar and how they are different. Do the same by comparing Nigel's Dad's garden shed and your classroom.

Categorising

This is a kind of grouping. So blackcurrants, blackberries, gooseberries and plums could all be categorized as types of fruit. However, 'fruit' fits into the larger category of flowering plants, which itself fits into the larger category of 'plants', which is nested inside the category of 'living things'. Nigel has a pet cat called Leo. Do some research into how Leo can be categorized or classified. In other words, what are the nested categories between 'Leo' and 'living things'?

Pick some items that are in your classroom that can be fitted into the same category. For example, pen, pencil and tablet are all implements used for writing.

Comparing

This focuses on both the similarities *and* differences between things. Create three lists as in this example comparing gooseberries with blackberries –

Blackberries only (differences) – dark purple or black, composed of many little parts (called drupelets) each containing a seed, grow in clusters, grow on runners, ripen late summer-early autumn.
Blackberries and gooseberries (similarities) – are fruits, are edible, similar size, have hairs on them, change colour as they ripen.
Gooseberries only (differences) – green or yellowy-green, each composed of a single fruit, grow on bushes.

Again, pick a couple of items in the classroom that are similar in one or more ways. Make a list of their similarities but also of how they differ.

Pick two characters from a story you know and compare them, noting similarities and differences.

Ordering in Terms of Size

This is self-explanatory. Here's a list of terms related to language. Put them in the correct order from smallest to largest –

Novel, phoneme, sentence, chapter, phrase, paragraph, letter, word, syllable, scene, trilogy.

Now order these shapes in terms of how many sides they have, from fewer to greater (you may need to do some research) –

Square, octagon, heptagon, triangle, decahedron, pentagon, dodecagon, nonagon, hendecagon.

All of these shapes fit into the category of polygons (from the Greek meaning 'many angled'). You may want to research where some of the other names come from. Incidentally, a polygon exists called a chiliagon that has 1,000 sides!

Things can be ordered according to time as well such as dawn, midday, afternoon, dusk, night. Find another category that can be ordered by time, jumble up the items and pass them to a friend to put them into time-related order.

Work with a few classmates to find a few other categories used for ordering.

Thinking about Concepts

A concept is an idea, often a generalised one. The word comes from the notion of 'taking into or appearing in the mind'. We use concepts all the time, without really thinking about them. Take the example of a clock. If you can see a clock in the classroom, then the concept – what you think about it – is of that particular clock, but the *notion* of 'clock' as it applies to all clocks is a general one. In both cases though the concept is a 'concrete' one because it refers to actual physical objects. The concept of 'time', however, is abstract – meaning it exists only as a thought or an idea. You might have come across this when learning about concrete and abstract nouns. Take a look at these sentences and in each case turn the word in italics (concrete noun) into an abstract noun at the end –

1 A *hero* gains respect because of her _____
2 A *child* goes to school throughout his _____
3 A *slave* has to suffer years of _____
4 A *coward* is looked down on for his _____
5 A *friend* is valued for her _____

The themes in narratives, both fiction and non-fiction, are often abstract concepts. In 'Crossing the Line', for example, we find the themes of –

Morality – the Double Darers understand it's wrong to steal Jones's fruit but they do it anyway.
Theft – the actual act of stealing the fruit.
Friendship – the Double Darers liking and looking out for each other.
Kindness – when Jones gives each of the children some of his fruit.
Remorse – given that the Double Darers apologise to Old Man Jones and take time to help him in his allotment.

Activity: Choose a story you've enjoyed and list some of its themes. Working as a whole class, are there any themes that are common to all the stories chosen by you and your classmates?

Activity: Think about some of the items currently in the news. Can you identify any of the themes behind those stories?

Activity: Some of the major themes in science (which is itself a concept or web of concepts) are: evolution, ecology, structure linked to function, inheritance, energy, science and society. Research any of these ideas that you don't understand. Can you think of any other concepts found in science, or in a particular branch of science?

Some abstract concepts or themes are common to many myths also, reinforcing the idea that myths are stories that 'tell us something true'. Such concepts include: fate, pride, heroism, justice, vengeance, beauty, love, loyalty, trust and many others.

Activity: Think about myths, legends, parables or folktales that you know, or can research, and identify some of the themes you find there. Ask your classmates what themes they've thought about. Are any of them common to all the examples the class has found?

Creating concepts – behind concepts are the properties or qualities that combine to make them. This is easier to understand by taking a physical object; let's use 'fruit', which is an important idea in 'Crossing the Line'.

'Fruit' is a general concept, a kind of catch-all idea that includes every kind of fruit. (By the way, to do the next activity, you might find it useful to look up what actually counts as a fruit.)

Activity: To investigate the concept of fruit, work in a group to list all the properties you can think of that apply to 'fruit'. So you might include: skin, juice, seeds or pips, hairs, stalk, edible, living thing, grows.

Now get rid of any properties that don't apply to every kind of fruit – or every kind that you can think of. Gooseberries and blackberries have hairs for example, but apples and bananas don't, so 'hairs' would be taken off the list.

Concepts that feature properties common to all examples within that concept help us to form robust (strong) definitions of it. But don't just accept definitions without thinking about them. In botany, for instance, we learn that 'fruit' is defined as 'vegetable products fit for food' (Concise Oxford Dictionary), or 'the sweet and fleshy product of a tree or other plant that contains seed and can be eaten as food' (Oxford Languages). However, thinking further would lead to us querying these definitions. In everyday language, we talk of shopping for fruit and vegetables: behind that is the notion that these two things are different. And yet in botany we learn that fruits and vegetables belong to the plant kingdom. Also, thinking botanically, we discover that a fruit is a seed-bearing structure that develops from the ovary of a flowering plant, while all the other parts of the plant, such as leaves, roots and stems, are classed as vegetables.

However, there's more to it than that. Looking again at the idea that fruits are 'vegetable products fit for food', a little research reveals that many fruits are inedible – Wikipedia for instance lists dozens of them.

And a moment's thought allows us to realise that the definition of fruit as 'the sweet and fleshy product of a tree or other plant that contains seed and can be eaten as food' makes the same error; limes and lemons, both fruits, are anything but sweet.

The lessons we can learn here are –

Just because something is written down in a book or online doesn't make it true.

Don't just accept ideas as facts, but question, check and check again.

Especially in the sciences, facts can become outdated very quickly. When you check ideas and definitions in science, use up-to-date sources of information, and look at more than one source.

Optional activity: Find a science book that's a number of years old. Pick a few facts from it and check them against the most recent information (remembering to check in at least a couple of places).

Abstract Concepts

These include all of our emotions.

Activity: Make a list of emotions such as kindness, anger, regret, anxiety, etc. (i.e. write them like that, as abstract nouns). Pick a few and write your own definitions of them. Then check your definition against others you find in a dictionary or online.

For example, our definition of kindness is 'doing something for another person with them in mind; being considerate, showing friendship'. Other definitions we came across include: the quality of being warm-hearted, considerate, humane and sympathetic, and of gentle and benevolent (well-meaning) nature, friendly, affectionate (showing fondness or tenderness).

However, if we think further about this, we come up with examples that test these definitions. If we give money to a homeless person on the street, would that be showing friendship? Would it show affection? If not it means that two of the definitions don't apply everywhere, 'The quality of being warm-hearted and considerate and humane and sympathetic' more accurately fits the bill. We learn from this that the definition of an emotion can change according to the particular situation when that emotion is expressed.

Not all abstract concepts are emotions in themselves, although many will have emotions associated with them. 'Success', for instance, is an abstract idea. If you succeed at something – think of an example – what emotions do you feel? But thinking of 'Democracy' – government by the people – it's more difficult to pin emotions on to the idea (though people living in a democracy might feel grateful that they do).

Generalising

Many concepts are generalisations. 'Gooseberry' for example doesn't refer to any particular gooseberry but includes all examples of that fruit. 'Success' too is a general (and abstract) concept that suggests but doesn't refer to any particular kind of success, or in what context. Generalisations are a useful sort of shorthand but care needs to be taken, especially when thinking about people, not to stereotype; in other words not to label whole groups of people based on one or a few examples. So if we came across a bad-tempered librarian in our local library, to think that 'librarians are bad tempered' would be to create an unfair and inaccurate stereotype (also see page 109).

One way of dampening this habit is to think 'some but not all' – the writer Robert Anton Wilson coined the term 'sombunall' based on this. So, 'sombunall (some but not all) librarians are bad tempered'. To think like this, in a more reasonable and less generalised way, is a skill that needs to be practised. You need to *notice* when you or somebody else stereotypes a group of people and deliberately follow it up by thinking 'sombunall'. Another way of challenging a generalisation is to think, 'but I don't *know* all librarians to be able to say that librarians generally are bad tempered'.

Decision-making

We make decisions all the time, some minor ones like which story to read next; some huge, like what career to aim for. Some decisions are based on hunches, whims or feelings, but others can be the outcome of a deliberate process of thinking. In other words, decision-making is also a thinking skill.

Referring back to our Double Darers story, suppose that another character, Ramesh, wanted to join the group: he's quite shy and doesn't have many friends. He's considering how to get the Darers to like him before he asks if he can join the group. Some of his ideas are –

I can pay the Double Darers to like me.
I can buy them sweets.
I can tell them some jokes.
I can offer to help them with their homework.
I can just hang around nearby and hope they notice me.

Help Ramesh to come to the best decision by taking the following steps –
List what you think are the good and bad points for each choice.

Think of any relevant ways of comparing these alternatives. In Ramesh's case, can he afford to pay the Double Darers? Is he too shy to tell them jokes, and would the Darers find them funny anyway? Is he good enough at his school subjects to help the Darers with their homework? We don't know the answers to these, but think about the consequences if the answer is either yes or no for each example and how asking that would bring him closer to a decision.

Now rate each choice on a 1–5 scale for at least one reason you've thought about; the word 'because' is useful here. So 'I can pay the Double Darers to like me' would score 1 in our view because the Darers might take the money and still not be friends, or because they might want paying more than once, or because they might just pretend to be friends. Can true friendship ever be bought with money?

Decide now which, if any, course of action you think Ramesh should take. If you don't think any of the alternatives are very good, can you come up with any better ones?

Activity: Here are four possible choices of career: teacher, shop owner, writer, doctor. (It doesn't matter whether you would choose any of these careers yourself.) Write down what you consider to be the good things and then the bad things in each case. Go through the decision-making process as you did for Ramesh: did any particular career stand out above the others? If you do have a career in mind for yourself, have you considered the reasons behind your choice, and if so how strong do you think those reasons are?

Creative Consequences

Douglas Hill, the late writer of children's science fiction, once told us that the whole of SF is based on asking 'what if?' Running what-if sessions with the class using fictional and non-fictional contexts brings a number of benefits –

Helps children to better understand the motifs and conventions of fictional genres, which can enrich their own genre writing and sharpen their critical thinking when evaluating other authors' work.

Helps to consolidate and embed knowledge if the what-if is based on a non-fictional topic forming part of the curriculum, using such knowledge with a focus on problem-solving.

Fosters a questioning attitude but also a tolerance for other people's ideas and points of view.

Can develop emotional resourcefulness if the what-if is focused on personal feelings. (Children might want to keep their thoughts private in such cases and think ideas through for themselves.)

Boosts both creative and critical thinking.

Stories and Learning   161

Note that even fictional what-ifs can lead to discussion of 'real world' issues and problems. For instance, we once ran this session with a Year Six class: What if human beings stopped growing once they reached adulthood and then started shrinking, so that by age 65 people were only 15 centimetres tall?
We appended these other questions to the scenario for guidance –

What would the world be like?
What problems would we have?
How could we solve those problems?

As well as coming up with inventions such as Perspex-covered walkways along the street to protect tiny older people, and small houses for pensioners (giving 'downsizing' a whole new meaning), the children showed great insight and empathy when it came to considering the needs, in this case, of older people.
Although you can offer the class what-if scenarios of your own, invite the children to come up with some too. In the past we've had –

What if dinosaurs still existed?
What if aliens invaded the Earth?
What if time travel was possible?
What if magic was real?

Many what-ifs that children suggest are based on stories they've read or watched. If a child offers a scenario, encourage the class to ask her questions about it before launching the what-if. In the case of magic, classmates wanted to know if it could be used for evil purposes as well as good ones; if magic became stronger the more you practised it; if people were born with a certain amount of magic and when it was gone it was gone; whether the magic was contained in people, in objects (like a wand), or in both; and could people give their own magic away to others?
If the child offering the what-if struggles to answer any of the questions, invite brief discussions to come up with acceptable ideas.
Tip: Comics are a great source of what-ifs, such as being able to go invisible, change size, fly, have super strength, etc.

Activity: What-ifs and written forms.
First, we want to make a distinction between the form that a piece of writing can take and the genre of a piece of fiction as we defined it earlier. By forms we mean things like story, poem, letter, journal, report, essay, email, newspaper article, blog, radio play, text message and comic strip. Genres include Science Fiction, Fantasy, Horror, Thriller,

etc. Some sources use the term 'genre' to mean forms, but we want to keep the two ideas separate.

Once children have explored a what-if, any written outcomes can take different forms. If the class discussed the what-if of dinosaurs living today, one child might write a newspaper report about dinosaurs escaping from 'Cretaceous Park', another could write a poem about an encounter with a Triceratops and so on. If children prefer to draw, they could create a comic strip of an incident, design an advertisement using dinosaurs, etc.

Finally, and in line with the title of this section, running what-if sessions encourages children to think about the future, to consider the consequences of how we act today, both individually and collectively. Some such future-focused speculations can also have a 'visionary' feel to them, conjuring up wide-ranging scenarios of what the world and humanity might be like decades, centuries or even millennia from now.

Teaching as Storytelling

Professor Kieran Egan, who we met earlier (pages 62 and 94), in his book 'Teaching as Storytelling' (Egan, 1989) suggests an alternative to the orthodox model of objectives-content-methods-evaluation way of planning lessons. His focus is on using narrative structure as a template for structuring lessons which, he says, utilises the power of children's imaginations and the fact that children are readily engaged by stories, not least because of their emotional impact. In other words, Egan is saying that even from a very early age, children understand story structure, however implicitly; that they have the 'conceptual tools' to follow and appreciate a narrative – obviously ones pitched at their age range. (This resonates with Bruno Bettelheim's suggestion to simply tell children fairy tales without explaining them, because at some level children come to understand their narrative structure – page 56).

The primary features of Kieran Egan's model are the use of binary opposites (good/bad, courage/cowardice, fear/security, for instance) and affective meaning; how emotional force is essential in how stories engage us. This has long been recognised: it was Plato who said that 'Reason must have an adequate emotional base for education to perform its function'. Further, that telling a story is a way of establishing meaning.

The story form model follows these steps in planning a lesson or topic –

Identifying importance: What is most important about this topic? In other words, what are the primary meanings and messages that children should take away from the lesson, because such meanings are relevant to their lives? Also, what is 'affectively engaging' about the lesson: What emotions may be evoked in learners that draw them into the story?

Finding binary opposites: What opposing or conflicting themes/concepts best catch the importance of the topic?

Organising the content into story form, by selecting content that most dramatically captures the binary opposites and helps to organise the content into narrative form.

Conclusion/resolution: What aspects of the topic content best resolves the dramatic conflict built into the story/topic?

Evaluation: How can we evaluate whether the topic has been understood and its importance grasped?

It would be wrong of us to simplify, therefore possibly misrepresenting, the elegance of Professor Egan's model: we said at the start of this book that one of our aims was to point the way to other resources that can help to develop children's understanding of narrative, and 'Teaching as Storytelling' will certainly help to achieve this. In his book, Egan puts 'flesh on the bones' by showing how the storytelling model works in various subject areas and across a range of topics, from communities, to Vikings, to Communism Vs Capitalism, counting and the use of the decimal system, to comma use and, more broadly, the accurate use of grammar and syntax.

In this last example, the importance of the lesson, as far as the children are concerned, is the expression of one's own individuality through writing. We can argue that everyone wants to develop a healthy sense of self-identity and that one way of communicating that is through writing clearly and with an individual voice. Egan is keen that one of the messages children should take away from the lesson is that there is a danger that the routine use of the rules and conventions of writing can lead to 'bland uniformity', the very opposite of an individual style.

The binary opposites of the lesson are therefore identified as vivid individuality and what Egan calls 'dull conventionality'. Our interpretation of this is that the development of a writer's individual voice, which requires the challenge of hard work and perseverance, represents the hero's journey, while the 'villain' of the piece is relative ignorance of grammar and syntax, coupled with not caring if one's writing might be judged as dry and merely utilitarian.

The content of such a lesson can be embedded in narrative form, Egan suggests, by showing the class two letters. One is written conventionally, 'with all the formulas of regards and hope-you-are-wells', while the other is quirky, individual and sprinkled with vivid details. In other words, in this second letter, the personality of the writer shines through. Egan also emphasises that the letter could be structured as a piece with a beginning that states the purpose for writing, a middle that recounts one or more incidents in the child's life and an ending that rounds off what the child wants to say.

Activity: Set the class the task of writing a letter or email or text message, to a real person or a fictional character, that lets each writer's personality shine through. You can suggest this without, at this stage, going into any detail about the narrative structure that Kieran Egan is outlining. Also, you might give the children a little time to reflect on how they would describe their own personalities, and then discuss in a general way what could go into a letter to give it a distinctive style and voice.

A variation of the activity is to suggest to half the class that they should make their letters as accurate as possible with regard to spelling, punctuation and grammar, while the other half is instructed to 'just have fun' by making their letters as quirky and interesting as possible. Note that this is not to devalue technical accuracy, but to make the point that letting one's personality shine through is at least as important as spelling, etc., which can be tidied up at the revising stage.

The lesson can conclude with the children letting each other read their letters (within the positive and supportive ethos that exists in the classroom), commenting on and appreciating their individual quirkiness and how children have achieved this, and how these letters compare with the technically accurate ones (the writers of which might choose to write another letter showing more of their personalities).

Egan makes the point that because emotional engagement is one of the key features of the story form model, evaluating the lesson solely through the accuracy of children's writing in a conventional way is inadequate, but that trying to measure style and individual voice is more difficult …

Activity: Ask the children to look again at a published story by an author they really like. What is it about that writer's style that makes it individual? (Point out that we're not necessarily looking for a preferred genre, but more subtle aspects of the story such that you *know* it's written by J. K. Rowling or Julia Donaldson or whoever, even if you were presented with a single page that didn't mention any characters or particular places.)

One aspect of the evaluation of children's work is asking how much any child enjoyed writing their letter and what they can tell you of what they understand about writing (including comma use) that they didn't understand before.

Effective Learners

Developing children's understanding of narrative structure, together with all of its associated ways of thinking, will help many children to become more effective learners. Education is not just about accumulating information – the low-level ability to recall and reiterate facts – but knowing how to use information to gain insights, deepen understanding and generate fresh ideas. This becomes even more imperative given that today's children are growing up in a world of increasing complexity, and one where misinformation, disinformation, fake news, conspiracy theories and various kinds of persuasion are proliferating: the biologist E. O. Wilson feels that in today's world we are 'drowning in information and starved for wisdom'. Added to this is the assertion by Postman and Weingartner that we are 'walking encyclopedias of outdated information'. Ironically, in light of this, their book 'Teaching as a Subversive Activity' was first published in 1968, but much of what they say there is as relevant today as it was all those years ago.

Activity: Show children a world map from decades ago and compare it with an up-to-date one. And/or compare an old science book with one recently published.

We agree with Postman and Weingartner that effective learners –

Have confidence in their ability to learn, given that they are equipped with a raft of 'how-to' techniques for engaging with information critically/analytically and creatively.

Relish engaging with problems, meaning that a curriculum that brings problem-solving in a range of contexts and subject areas to the fore (rather than just the recollection of facts) is an environment in which children will thrive.

Are tolerant of ambiguity and uncertainty, this trait being linked to the fact that problems don't come bundled with pat solutions. Those solutions need to be worked out, so effective learners will also be reflective and willing to take time to consider alternatives. Coupled with this, effective learners are not fearful of wrong answers, seeing these as necessary steps on the path to the 'right' answers, i.e. the most relevant, appropriate or effective solutions, an attitude reflected by Albert Einstein who said, 'I have tried ninety-nine times and failed, but on the hundredth time came success'. As an adjunct to this, such children are not afraid to say, 'I don't know but how can I find out?' It's worth mentioning that reading stories fosters the attitude of tolerating ambiguity and uncertainty, insofar as children won't know how the central problem is resolved until near the end.

Give thought to what is relevant or irrelevant in terms of their education, which is the platform on which to build a successful and fulfilling life. In many cases, this is combined with a tolerance of those aspects of schooling they feel not be to so relevant, except insofar that they are steps on the journey to gaining the qualifications necessary to progress further.

Effective learners also appreciate that learning doesn't stop with the end of formal education; that learning and the search for relevance and meaning is indeed a lifelong quest.

E. O. Wilson, mentioned earlier, argues forcefully for the importance of including and valuing the Humanities within the curriculum since art (including literature), languages, philosophy, history, archaeology, anthropology, human geography, law and theology allow us to search for meaning through 'the infinity of all fantasy worlds'; that is, wherever the human imagination can take us. He feels that because of this, the Humanities encompass the fields of scientific observation, which addresses all phenomena existing in the real world; scientific experimentation, which addresses all possible real worlds; and scientific theory, which addresses all conceivable real worlds. As such, the Humanities go beyond science and offer us other and diverse ways of finding meaning, personal or general, within the universe as a lifelong quest.

Education consultant and author Mike Tilling reinforces these points in his 'Adventures in Learning' (Tilling, 2001). Tilling uses the template of the hero's quest as a metaphor for children's education (see also Kieran Egan's 'Teaching as Storytelling' on page 162) and touches on the notion of 'deep learners'. He identifies such learners as children who –

Look for meaning.
Want to interact actively with the subject matter.
Link learning with their own lives (by searching for relevancy).
Are prepared to change their beliefs and attitudes in light of new information.
Assimilate new knowledge into what they already know.
Examine evidence carefully and critically.
Enjoy learning for its own sake.

We can recognise here characteristics that fit with the 'higher levels' of Bloom's Taxonomy of thinking as explored on page 138). Tilling contrasts deep learners with what he calls 'surface' learners, who tend to –

Over-emphasise the importance of rote learning.
Be particularly conscious of and concerned by assessments and examinations[†].
Want to accumulate 'facts' (what Tilling calls the Mastermind concept of learning).
Have difficulty making creative connections between concepts.
Be passive and uncritical recipients of information.
View learning as a means to an end.

† Steve – I remember working with a group that had just entered Year Six. As the children wrote in response to a task I'd set, I wandered around the room to offer help if needed. I happened to say to one boy, 'So, are you enjoying Year Six?' He shook his head and said, 'No, I'm worrying about the SATs'. 'Nuff said', as they say in the comics.

The traits of effective/deep learners are reflected in the fact that such children are competent in different 'language environments', realising that language can obscure differences and control perceptions, a point echoed by Postman and Weingartner; that perception is a function of the linguistic categories available to the perceiver. Margaret Meek (page 3) also urges educators to work towards helping children to become more 'critically literate', while Alexander Eliot feels that the dispositions for effective learning are creative imagination, intellect and 'emotional force' (what we take to mean passion).

The 'how-to' that helps learners to achieve these can be embodied in a number of questions for reflecting on whatever 'language environment' needs to be explored and assessed, whether this is the language of myth, science, history, news reporting, advertising, politics and so on, and the narratives that such language conveys ...

What are the underlying purposes of this language context?

What are its major assumptions?

From which point of view are the narratives being communicated?

What are some of the key terms being used within this form of language?

What are its most important symbols and metaphors?

What values does this language environment embody?

What beliefs does this use of language want me to accept? What persuasive tactics are being used?

What standards can I apply to test the truth? So how does 'political truth' differ from 'scientific truth', from 'philosophical truth', etc.? Are there any aspects of these 'truths' that they have in common?

Staying a little longer with the relationship between language and perception, Postman and Weingartner make some cogent points –

Perceptions are created within our own minds; that our experiences and the meanings we make of them rest on our system of values and beliefs, which serve us best when we think critically about how any language context is trying to influence us. Another aspect of this idea is that the flexibility with which we can influence our own perceptions is correlated with the range of linguistic categories available to us. The more we encourage the understanding of narrative structure in children by getting them to question, analyse, challenge assumptions, understand metaphors, recognise rhetorical/persuasive tactics, etc. and the 'stories' these contribute to, the more they'll develop the wherewithal to influence their own perceptions and literally 'make up their own minds'.

We are less likely to alter our perceptions until we find ourselves frustrated in our attempts to achieve something based upon them, i.e. until there is a conflict between our purposes and the assumptions we've made within a given language environment. One characteristic of the effective learner is to challenge her own perceptions and have the creative nous to generate possible alternatives – back to Kieran Egan's ironic understanding (page 61).

Since we create our own perceptions of what's out there in the world, at least in the sense of giving personal meaning to what we experience, each of us is unique in perceiving what the world is like (a personal world view superimposed on what we might call consensus reality. We can both agree that a table is a table, but you might love a table because you made it yourself and I might loathe it because it reminds me of a table I fell off once and nearly broke my neck. What was I doing on the table? You'll never know.). One important ramification of this idea is the willingness of a critically thinking person to listen respectfully to the viewpoints of others, but to assess them and come to one's own conclusions. For example, the poet Gerard Manley Hopkins (page 49) felt that, 'the world is charged with the grandeur of God', whereas the biologist Richard Dawkins believes that, 'The universe that we observe has precisely the properties we should expect if there is, at bottom, no design, no purpose, no evil and no good, nothing but blind, pitiless indifference'. Clearly, these beliefs reflect radically different world views. The idea is neatly summed up in the aphorism that, 'we see the world, not as it is, but as we are' (attributed to various people).

Finally, the meaning of a perception is reflected in how it causes us to act. We might agree that the sun is shining, but if Steve has an aversion to sitting out in the sun, while Tony really enjoys working on his tan (he likes to be beach-body ready), then our perceptions of 'the sun is shining' are obviously different and will affect how we react to the fact of the sunny day.

We appreciate that at least some of these concepts will be beyond the understanding of many of the younger children within the target age range of this book; but as educators, we feel we should consider them ourselves and, as far as possible, lead our children towards being able to tackle them.

Endwords

First, though you have probably already had this thought, we want to say that the ideas we've offered in this book reflect our own set of values, beliefs, opinions and – yes indeed – our own biases too. There is of course so much more that could be said about the links between narrative and myth, science, the media, etc. but we have tried to offer you a selection of ideas that amount to our own 'stories' behind these different fields. So, for example, we approve of Rupert Sheldrake's mission to challenge scientific orthodoxy (page 90), whereas another author writing about science might condemn it as an attempt to subvert science and rationality. We trust, then, that you will take this into account when using what we have said to inform both yourself and your pupils.

On a broader note, Don Watson in 'Gobbledygook' rightly says that language is our most valuable cultural inheritance but, referring to the basic narrative elements, it can be the hero or the villain in one's life. As Matthew D'Ancona asserts in 'Post Truth', narrative must never violate or embellish truth; it should be its most powerful vehicle. But how often though does narrative indeed violate or embellish truth, and in so many different and often subtle ways? The noted biologist E. L. Grant Watson in 'The Mystery of Physical Life' (Grant Watson, 1992) brings this point directly into the classroom by asserting that 'since most students believe what they are taught ... some apply their belief(s) to their general outlook'. Neil Postman and Charles Weingartner insist that being illiterate in any medium leaves one at the mercy of those who control it; hence the need to develop children's willingness to question when cultivating their critical and creative thinking abilities and their intelligence in general – although we would go beyond this to suggest that intelligence (from the Latin 'to understand') leads to wisdom (from Old English meaning learned, sagacious, cunning; sane; prudent, discreet; experienced; having the power of discerning and judging rightly). Thus, our primary aim through this book has been to show how you can develop children's understanding of narrative in order for them to become 'StoryWise'.

* * *

Bibliography

Note that these are the editions we used in our research. More recent editions may be available. Also, all references are to physical editions; digital editions may also exist.

Aaronovitch, D. Voodoo Histories: how conspiracy theory has shaped modern history. London: Vintage, 2010.
Benson, R. Everything You Think You Know Is Wrong: exposing the truth behind common myths and misconceptions. London: Summersdale Publishers, 2018.
Bettelheim, B. The Uses of Enchantment. London: Penguin Books, 1991.
Bierce, A. The Enlarged Devil's Dictionary. London: Penguin Books, 1989.
Birch, H., Looi, M. K. & Stuart, C. The Big Questions in Science. London: SevenOaks, 2017.
Bowkett, S. Developing Self-confidence in Young Writers. London: Bloomsbury, 2017.
Bowkett, S. & Hitchman, T. Developing Thinking Skills Through Creative Writing: story steps for 9-12 year-olds. Abingdon, Oxon: Routledge, 2020.
Bowkett, S. & Hitchman, T. Visualising Literacy and How To Teach It: a guide to developing thinking skills, vocabulary and imagination for 9-12 year-olds. Abingdon, Oxon: Routledge, 2022.
Bowkett, S. with Hogston, K. Jumpstart! Wellbeing. Abingdon, Oxon: Routledge, 2017.
Bowkett, S. Jumpstart! Philosophy in the Classroom. Abingdon, Oxon: Routledge, 2018.
Brooks, M. 13 Things That Don't Make Sense. London: Profile Books, 2010.
Brunvand, J. H. The Vanishing Hitchhiker: urban legends and their meanings. London: Pan Books, 1983.
Brunvand, J. H. Curses! Broiled Again! New York, NY: W. W. Norton & Company, 1990.
Brunvand, J. H. Be Afraid, Be Very Afraid: the book of scary urban legends. New York, NY: W. W. Norton and Co., 2004.
Brush, N. The Limitations of Scientific Truth. Grand Rapids, MI: Kregel, 2005.
Buckley, J. Pocket P4C. Chelmsford: One Slice Books, 2011.
Campbell, J. with Boa, F. The Way of Myth. Boston, Mass: Shambala, 1994.
Campbell, J. with Moyers, B. The Power of Myth. New York, NY: Anchor Books, 1988.

Canetti, E. Crowds and Power. New York, NY: Farrar, Straus and Giroux, 1984.
Carter, C. Science and Psychic Phenomena: the fall of the house of skeptics. Rochester, Vermont: Inner Traditions, 2012.
Ceram, C. W. Gods, Graves and Scholars: the story of archaeology. Harmondsworth, Middlesex: Penguin, 1974.
Chetwynd, T. Dictionary of Symbols. London: HarperCollins, 1982.
Clarke, A. C. 2001 A Space Odyssey. London: Arrow Books, 1970.
Cohen, M. 101 Ethical Dilemmas. London: Routledge, 2004.
Collins, H. & Pinch, T. The Golem: what you should know about science. Cambridge: Cambridge University Press, 2003.
D'Ancona, M. Post Truth: the new war on truth and how to fight back. London: Ebury Press, 2017.
Daniken, E. von, Chariots of the Gods: was God an astronaut? London: Corgi Books, 1971.
Danser, S. The Myths of Reality. Loughborough, Leicestershire: Alternative Albion, 2005.
De Botton, A. The News: a user's manual. London: Hamish Hamilton, 2014.
De Vos, G. Tales, Rumors and Gossip. Englewood, CO: Libraries Unlimited Inc., 1996.
Dweck, C. S. Self-theories: their role in motivation, personality and development. New York, NY: Psychology Press, 2000.
Egan, K. Teaching as Story Telling. Chicago, IL: University of Chicago Press, 1989.
Egan, K. The Educated Mind: how cognitive tools shape our understanding. Chicago, IL: The University of Chicago Press, 1998.
Egan, K. Learning in Depth: a simple innovation that can transform schooling. Chicago, IL: University of Chicago Press, 2011.
Ekwall, E. The Concise Oxford Dictionary of Place Names. Oxford: Oxford University Press, 1981.
Eliot, A. The Universal Myths. Harmondsworth, Middlesex: Penguin Books, 1990.
Eliot, A. The Timeless Myths. Harmondsworth, Middlesex: Penguin Books, 1997.
Evans, A. The Myth Gap: what happens when evidence and argument aren't enough? London: Eden Project Books, 2017.
Gardner, W. H. (Ed.), Gerard Manley Hopkins: poems and prose. Harmondsworth, Middlesex: Penguin Books, 1970.
Garrett, R. Hoaxes and Swindles. London: Piccolo, 1978.
Garvey, J. The Persuaders: the hidden industry that wants to change your mind. London: Icon Books, 2016.
Geary, J. I Is an Other: the secret life of metaphor and how it shapes the way we see the world. New York, NY: HarperCollins, 2011.
Goldberg, P. The Intuitive Edge: understanding and developing intuition. Wellingborough, Northants: Crucible, 1989.
Goss, M. The Evidence for Phantom Hitch-Hikers. Wellingborough, Northants: The Aquarian Press, 1984.
Grant Watson, E. L. The Mystery of Physical Life. Edinburgh: Floris Books, 1992.
Hittleman, R. Guide to Yoga Meditation. New York, NY: Bantam Books, 1969.

Jaynes, J. The Origin of Consciousness in the Breakdown of the Bicameral Mind. London: Penguin Books, 1993.

Kuhn, T. S. The Structure of Scientific Revolutions. London: The University of Chicago Press, 1970.

Law, S. The Philosophy Files 1 & 2. London: Orion Children's Books, 2002 & 2003.

Laws, P. The Frighteners: why we love monsters, ghosts, death & gore. London: Icon Books, 2018.

Le Bon, G. The Crowd. New York, NY: Ballantine Books, 1969.

Le Fanu, J. Why Us? How Science Rediscovered the Mystery of Ourselves. London: HarperPress, 2010.

Mackay, C. Extraordinary Delusions and the Madness of Crowds. Ware, Herts: Wordsworth, 1995.

May, R. The Cry for Myth. London: Souvenir Press, 1993.

Medawar, P. The Limits of Science. Oxford: Ixford University Press, 1986.

Meek, M. On Being Literate. London: Bodley Head, 1991.

Meyer, R. The Wisdom of Fairy Tales. Edinburgh: Floris Books, 1988.

Murray, H. A. (Ed.), Myth and Mythmaking. Boston, Mass.: Beacon Press, 1968.

Plait, Philip. Bad Astronomy. New York, NY: John Wiley & Sons, 2002.

Postman, N. & Weingartner, C. Teaching as a Subversive Activity. Harmondsworth, Middlesex: Penguin Books, 1972.

Price, B. Unsolved Science. London: New Burlington Books, 2016.

Propp, V. Morphology of the Folktale. Austin, Texas: University of Texas Press, 2001.

Pryor, F. Flag Fen: life and death of a prehistoric landscape. Stroud, Glos: The History Press, 2015.

Randles, J. Truly Weird: real life cases of the paranormal. London: Collins & Brown, 1998.

Randles, J., Roberts, A. & Clarke, D. The UFOs That Never Were. London: London House, 2000.

Reps, P. Zen Flesh, Zen Bones. Harmondsworth, Middlesex: Penguin Books, 1980.

Rockett, M. & Percival, S. Thinking for Learning. Stafford: Network Educational Press, 2002.

Root-Bernstein, R. & M. Honey Mud Maggots and Other Medical Marvels: the science behind remedies and old wives' tales. London: Macmillan, 1999.

Rosenthal, R. & Jacobson, L. Pygmalion in the Classroom: teacher expectation and pupils' intellectual development. New York, NY: Irvington Publishers Inc., 1992.

Saunders, A. Apollo Remastered. London: Particular Books/Penguin, 2022.

Schick, N. Deep Fakes and the Infocalypse: what you urgently need to know. London: Monoray, 2020.

Schneiderman, K. Step Out of Your Story. Novato, CA: New World Library, 2015.

Sheldrake, R. A New Science of Life. London: Paladin, 1985.

Sheldrake, R. The Science Delusion: freeing the spirit of enquiry. London: Coronet, 2012.

Shenkman, R. Legends, Lies and Cherished Myths of World History. New York, NY: HarperCollins, 1993.
Story, R. The Space Gods Revealed. London: Book Club Associates, 1977.
Sullivan, J. W. N. The Limitations of Science. New York, NY: Mentor Books, 1961.
Sunderland, M. Using Story Telling as a Therapeutic Tool with Children. Bicester, Oxon: Winslow, 2000.
Thompson, M. Teach Yourself Philosophy of Science. London: Hodder Headline, 2006.
Tilling, M. Adventures in Learning. Stafford: Network Educational Press, 2001.
Vardy, P. What is Truth: beyond postmodernism and fundamentalism Alresford, Hants. John Hunt, 2003.
Wallas, L. Stories for the Third Ear. London: W. W. Norton & Company, 1985.
Watson, D. Gobbledygook. London: Atlantic Books, 2005.
Webb, N. The Dictionary of Bullshit. London: Robson Books, 2005.
Webb, N. The Dictionary of Political Bullshit. London: JR Books, 2010.
Wilson, E. O. The Origins of Creativity. London: W. W. Norton & Company Limited, 2017.

Index

advertising 122; targeted at children 99
anchoring 135
anecdote 59
Apollo Moonshot Program 4
appeal to authority 76
argument from antiquity 96
atmosphere in stories 11, 41
authorial 'voice' 36, 163

bias 107, in history 102
Bloom's Taxonomy of thinking 138

Campbell, Joseph (American mythologist) 55
character 'types' (as opposed to stereotypes) 25
Clarke, Arthur C. (Science Fiction writer) 4, 36, 58, 79
cliché, 14, 16, 25, 34, 121
concepts 156, 158
concluding 141
confidence in writing 39, 165
conspiracy theories 116
creative consequences 160; *see also* What-if
creativity 31; the process of 57; and randomness 14
credulity 78
critical thinking 43, 62, 73, 79
'Crossing the Line' (exemplar story) 143
crowd behaviour 112

decision making 159
deep fakes 125
defining 158

Doctor Who (British TV series) 13, 17, 48
Dogma 89

effective learners 164
effective writing 32, 45
Egan, K. (educational philosopher) 60, 94, 162
emotions personifying 133
euphemism 119
evolution 93
exaggeration 63, 73, 153

facts 6, 47, 61
falsifiability as an aspect of scientific theories 94
falsifying (results of experiments) 98
fairy tales 58, 62; disapproval of 59
fiction as 'telling us something true' 6, 21, 47
folklore 68
forms of writing (as distinct from genres) 38
fringe science 98

generalisations 78, 108, 159
genre 15, 68
gossip 50, 52
gullibility 71, 97

help as a narrative element 11
hero 8
Hierarchy of Understandings 61
Hill, Douglas (children's author) 36, 160
historical revisionism 114
hoaxes 98

Hopkins, G. M. (Victorian poet) 49, 133
'hurrah' words 121
Hypothesis 98

inferring 28
information, checking the veracity of 2, relevance of 143
information literacy 2
inspiration 134
intelligence 69

journey as a narrative element 10

knowledge / power as a narrative element 11
koans (Zen puzzles) 66

Ladder to the Moon (hierarchical metaphor for stories) 52
language: clarity of 119; environments of 167
legend, definition of 48
lensing (a visualisation technique) 40
logical consistency in narrative 16, 24

materialism 59, 86
metacognition 129
metaphor 91, in science 93
metaphorical thinking 23
minimal writing strategy (for motivating reluctant writers) 39
models of reality 108
morality 47, 51, 156
motifs (constituent features of narrative) 11, 15, 64
multiple intelligence theory 1
mumbo jumbo 94
myth: definition of 2, 48; etymology of 47; the need for 49; personal 127
mythic fragments 47, 58
mythosphere (the whole mythical landscape) 58

narrative, definition of 1
narrative elements 8
narrative template 18
Neuro Linguistic Programming (NLP) 108
news 123
newspapers 107; names of 123; structure of articles 123

object(ive), as a narrative element 11
Occam's Razor (the principle of parsimony) 116

parable, definition of 66
paradigm 77, 87
partner, as a narrative element 10
person (1st, 2nd, 3rd) 37
persuasion 111, 165
persuasive tactics 112
place names 32
play 3
politics
post truth 115
problem as a narrative element 10
Pryor, Francis (Archaeologist) 36, 47, 101
pseudo-science 96
Pygmalion Effect (expectations influencing outcomes) 132

Questioning 43, 89

randomness in the creative process (story grids, polyhedral dice, two-colour counter) 14
rationality 56, 57
reality checking 125
reasoning 56, 76
reframing 131
relativism 2, 90, 115
relaxation techniques 129
rumours 52, 75

scientism 89
settings 32, 41
simile 91, 121, 153
sombunall ('some but not all') 78
stackers game 69
Star Wars ('a myth for the 20th Century') 10, 21, 55, 56
stereotypes 23, 86, 108, 159
story checklist (before and after writing) 44
story grids 14, 44, 63
story hill, planning tool 18
story 'ingredients' 15
story pyramid 6
storytelling 3, 21; possible origins 1
subconscious processing 56
sub-elements in narrative 13

supermarkets 114
superstition 78
symbols 22, 135

text, etymology of and links with 'textiles' 17
themes 3, 6, 8
thinking skills 63, 79, 140
thought experiment 67, 114
truth 49, 89, 90, 115
twenty questions game 43

Universal Grammar theory 68
urban folk tales 71

villain 9, 12, 18
visualising 129
vivid particularity (vivid mental image with emotional impact) 26

what-if (a form of speculation and thought experiment) 40, 160
wonderment 62

For Product Safety Concerns and Information please contact our EU representative GPSR@taylorandfrancis.com
Taylor & Francis Verlag GmbH, Kaufingerstraße 24, 80331 München, Germany

www.ingramcontent.com/pod-product-compliance
Lightning Source LLC
Chambersburg PA
CBHW051745230426
43670CB00012B/2170